HOW TO LEAVE TWITTER

How to Leave Twitter

*My Time as Queen of the Universe
and Why This Must Stop*

GRACE DENT

faber and faber

First published in this edition in 2011
by Faber and Faber Ltd
Bloomsbury House
74–77 Great Russell Street London WC1B 3DA
and
Guardian Books
Guardian Books is an imprint of Guardian Newspapers Ltd

A CIP record for this book
is available from the British Library

ISBN 978-0-571-27774-2

2 4 6 8 10 9 7 5 3 1

For Emma Kennedy

100 things about me and Twitter

1. My name is @gracedent.

2. I joined Twitter on 4 June 2008.

3. @febake was the first person to tell me about Twitter. It took him several months of preaching about its wonders until I cracked.

4. My first ever tweet was, 'looking puzzled at twitter.' No-one replied. I mooched off into cyberspace, humiliated.

5. I returned in early 2009 because my friend @heawood joined.

6. We swapped twitpics of bears in Victorian bonnets and insults about body-hair issues. I dumped all my surplus silly thoughts there about *EastEnders*, *Big Brother* and columns I couldn't be bothered to write.

7. By July 2009 I had about 5,987 followers.

8. Back then I said pretty much whatever I wanted on Twitter. It was like spraying rude words on a fence in neon, foot-high letters and never, ever getting detention for it.

9. Today on Twitter I feel like a slightly feral village elder. My teeth itch when people tweet me to tell me what I'm not allowed to say.

10. When @heawood moved to LA to interview movie stars, we kept in touch mainly via Twitter. I missed her so much I tweeted her YouTube links of sad songs.

11. Maudlin soft-rock ballad 'So Far Away' by Dire Straits was most effective. @heawood now lives back in London.

12. I check Twitter on my iPhone each day within five minutes of opening my eyes.

13. I have woken myself up in the middle of the night checking Twitter in my sleep.

14. I think I can tell if you are fibbing about being on Twitter within one minute of talking to you.

15. I think I can tell if a person has enough 'voice' to write a whole novel by simply reading a few tweets.

16. My most retweeted tweet was a profound quotation by Albert Camus rallying against nihilism.

17. That is a lie. It was a screen-grab of *X-Factor* boyband member Harry Styles looking like he had a massive erection.

18. My second most RT'd tweet was a scan of the under-carriage of a white cat with pink paws who had sat on a scanner machine.

19. I know people who monitor the success of every thought by its RT tally. I am not one of those people.

20. But if a tweet gets NO replies at all, it makes me edgy.

21. As I type this list I've got 54,851 followers.

22. As I type this list I've tweeted 27,325 times.

23. As I type this list I'm telling myself 90% of those 27,325 tweets were probably quick @replies to people and NOT actual posts in my timeline, because this makes it less of 'a problem'.

24. I use Twitter clients and apps like TweetDeck or Echofon. I suspect they give me migraines but I just take codeine and carry on, for how can I monitor the universe in real time without multiple columns?

25. Twitter definitely made me more well known. I'm not sure if it made me more well liked.

26. I once said on an ITV2 show that *X-Factor* contestant Stacey Solomon was 'not a terribly good singer' and had to leave Twitter for two weeks due to an angry twitchfork mob chasing me around cyberspace.

27. Grace Dent has been a 'trending topic' on a few occasions. It's not very nice really. It just opens you up to a global level of maniac.

28. Twitter led to me watching two weeks of all-night Olympic curling with @emmak67 and hundreds of other tweeters. I still do not understand curling. It still looks like Olympic-grade housework.

29. I've spent New Year's Eve on Twitter. It was better than going out.

30. Twitter led to me keeping an emergency picture of a member of the rock band Kiss sneaking to a festival Portaloo just to cheer Twitter buddies up.

31. Twitter led to @gracedent being close personal chums with the pop star Will Young.

32. After several direct-message exchanges it turned out not to be Will Young, just a man pretending to be him

while pulling furiously at his own penis. @gracedent was disappointed.

33. I often see that @gracedent has blocked someone 'for absolutely no reason'. There's ALWAYS been a reason.

34. I sometimes block tweeters who demand I retweet them without even saying hello first.

35. I sometimes unfollow tweeters for RTing praise about themselves.

36. I still class it as RTing praise if they've cunningly added 'THIS PERSON MUST BE MAD TO SAY THIS!!' on to the end of the tweet.

37. I once blocked @emmak67 during a row over politics to make the point that she was getting on my tits. Then due to a technical malfunction I couldn't unblock her for a week, which led to a month-long row.

38. I think the most boring tweets in the world are DJs' 'I'm at an airport' tweets.

39. Although any 'I have jetlag. Boo-hoo, I'll just order room service then' tweets are fractionally worse.

40. And I would love to punch the person in the throat who thinks it's a worthwhile task to set up a 'sausage' bot. Or a 'radiator' bot.

41. I love tweets featuring talking cats, snoring cats, cats jumping in boxes, cats jumping out of boxes, etc.

42. I think there's a strong pro-cat propaganda unit working on Twitter.

43. I think there's either a worldwide dearth of clips of dogs being idiots, or the pro-dog lobby needs to up its Twitter game.

44. I suck at Twitter hashtags games. I tend to sit those games out.

45. I bloody love Twitter 'pun' games. I'll play them until the bitter end, when my puns need brackets to explain and no-one replies.

46. I get arsey when non-Twitter people say Twitter is just people discussing their breakfasts. Only an idiot tweets their breakfast.

47. I do sometimes tweet about lunch.

48. Twitter has made me seriously wonder if chronic pedantry is a social illness. People are crucified by their need to correct commas.

49. I think if you cancel an appointment with me due to being busy or ill you should have the common sense to stop fucking tweeting.

50. I believe 3,000 followers is the point at which lots of tweeters start behaving like utter maniacs. '3,000 follower syndrome' is a worrying medical condition.

51. The first sign of '3,000 follower syndrome' is apologising for not checking in on Twitter until later than usual, believing that Twitter must have felt so empty without you.

52. The second sign is placing tweets in your timeline answering the question you say 'everyone' is asking you. If you check this person's @ column it almost invariably turns out no-one is speaking to them.

53. It gets even worse after that.

54. Twitter led to me chatting to Curt Smith from Tears for Fears. Me being the eleven-year-old @gracedent who has *Smash Hits* on order from the newsagents and thinks this is very cool.

55. @simonjclebon once tweeted @gracedent, but she was too shy to tweet back. @gracedent left him hanging.

56. I've left Twitter several times in a massive strop.

57. But I always, always come back.

58. I worry that I can never leave Twitter as normal life feels like wading through treacle.

59. I worry that I'm missing out if I don't check Twitter.

60. I worry that Twitter has killed my ability to focus on one thought for more than ten seconds.

61. I love it when other tweeters drastically announce they are leaving Twitter in a dramatic way. I call this 'dumbass digital suicide'.

62. I make rude noises at my screen when tweeters @ me to say they're unfollowing me. I'm not Moses, we weren't going to the Promised Land. Follow whoever you want.

63. I unfollow my friends all the time. I think life's too short to have someone pissing you off in your timeline. It's like radio interference in your brain on a lovely day.

64. I'm freaked out by people who use 'have you un-followed me' software to monitor who has digitally dumped them. Is there not enough pain in the world already?

65. I dread receiving the 'very terrible oh-why-have-you-unfollowed-me boo-hoo email of doom.'

66. I think we focus too much on celebrities' contributions to Twitter. Celebrities aren't the tweeters providing interesting content. I discard them and their third-rate Twitter jibber-jabber all the time.

67. I unfollowed @piersmorgan for reading out his follower account figures all the time and begging for more like a telethon.

68. I unfollowed @Lord_Sugar for RTing questions asking where we could buy his book.

69. I unfollowed @ladygaga as she drones on all day about her 'little monsters' like a saleswoman flogging U-bend germ-killer detergent.

70. I unfollowed @KimKardashian out of sheer pettiness because I like to believe I corner the market in 'brunettes with big arses who contribute very little to the world of entertainment'.

71. I unfollowed @rustyrockets after his stag do ended up in Stringfellows. I was on a militant feminist tip that day, someone was going to get it.

72. I unfollowed @50cent because the poor man is almost entirely fixated on the daily happenings of his own penis.

73. I unfollowed @BarackObama because it turns out being Mr President is a whole lot of paperwork. Mate, there's a reason I don't tweet my VAT return.

74. I send ten tweets a month to pop star Peter Andre giving him feedback about his career, but he never replies.

75. I hate the terms 'tweet-up' and 'twunk'.

76. I love the term 'twitchfork mob'.

77. When twitchfork mobs are circling some poor tweeter for crimes of thought I often add the rumour 'I heard he bummed a puffin' simply to cheer myself up.

78. I love the term 'twanking' (wanking while tweeting).

79. I get tweeted quite a lot of pictures of penises and offers of sex. 'I fink we should make a play date 4 our GENITILZ!' one man wrote just this very morning.

80. I get at least one unsolicited tweet a week from a stranger pointing out that in my current state of vast ugliness they'd never fuck me.

81. I think if one morning everyone's direct-message box was suddenly, accidentally posted in the public timeline there would be rioting in international cities by lunchtime. Most of this would be warring couples chucking bin-bags of clothes at each other.

82. I think most people don't realise that posting a photo on DM means EVERYONE who looks at your photo account can still see it. It's not private. I've seen two photos of my friends I wish I hadn't.

83. One of them was in the bath.

84. The other one was indescribable but it scarred my retinas.

85. I've seen perfectly good marriages go down the pan because of Twitter.

86. I genuinely cringe at my friends publicly arse-kissing each other on Twitter.

87. I find the way some people blatantly social-climb on Twitter vomit-making.

88. The phrase 'let's have a tweet-up' makes me nervous. I don't think meeting people off Twitter is necessary to be friends with them.

89. I never like Twitter 'tribute' sites where someone pretends to be someone else. I think they're usually one joke stretched very, very thinly in search of a toilet-book deal.

90. I know Twitter is the only place I can make jokes about my family, because, as of yet, they're not on Twitter. Once they join, it's all over.

91. I think the future of social networking lies in tackling the need for an individual to have 'multiple personalities' living easily on one social-networking platform. We are not one person all of the time, not even minute-to-minute.

92. I think there should be a meta-Twitter purely for gossiping about what we think other people are up to on Twitter.

93. At the moment I sometimes flip to Skype to chat face-to-face with friends about what we think the story is 'behind the tweets'. It's like *Minority Report*, but in pyjamas.

94. I get emails once a week from TV companies who say they want to 'harness the power of Twitter but ON TELEVISION'. They then fart around with meeting for ten weeks and realise it's fucking impossible.

95. This book is just a whole lot of my own personal thoughts, feelings and experiences of Twitter. I'm pretty certain you'll disagree with most of it.

96. I chatted to scores of people about Twitter as I was writing the book. Absolutely nobody agreed with anyone else's view on anything.

97. Everybody brought fresh angles and topics I'd never even thought of. I love this. Twitter is a totally different animal to everyone riding it.

98. I agreed to write *How to Leave Twitter* after a publishing meeting about a different book turned into an extended rant about RTs and Follow Fridays.

99. As I worked, I showed some parts of the manuscript to good friends, who went slightly ashen and said, 'Grace, you're going to break Twitter, you do know that, don't you?' In a way, this is brilliant. Killing Twitter is my only real chance of leaving.

100. I'd have delivered *How to Leave Twitter* to the publishing house a lot earlier and avoided a lot of stress and shouting matches, but in all honesty, I was too busy dicking about on the internet.

How to join Twitter

Every tweeter, no matter who they are, was a confused newbie at one point. I remember very clearly, in June 2008, staring at a virgin Twitter page, feeling awkward, silly and alone. Most of us went through a stage of refusing we even needed Twitter and, in fact, slagging it off. All classic behaviour. The road from grumpy refusenik to full-blown addict goes through several typical stages:

Pre-entry-level stage: resisting Twitter

1. Hear friends chatting about Twitter. Grunt: 'Uggh, Twitter? I've already got a Facebook and a dead Myspace page, and LinkedIn stalking my ass night and day. I'm NOT joining Twitter.'

2. Hear more hype about Twitter. Apparently it's communicating with people in under 140 characters, like the 'update' bar in Facebook. You hate that stupid update bar. Stare across office at Facebook-addicted colleague

picking at his teeth with a paperclip. (Zane's typical Facebook update: Zane Strang is eating a delicious peach and hoping Miss Ladybug's plane arrives safe.) Recall the time you unfriended Zane and the subsequent collateral damage as he boo-hoo-ed about it to everyone in the company.

3. Endure more Twitter evangelism. Dig your heels in. 'It's got a stupid name,' you say glibly to anyone not on Twitter left who cares. 'Twitter?!' you say. 'Like a bird tweeting inanely! It's for twits!' Believe you're the first person to have made this joke ever. Keep making it until someone shouts, 'Oh, get with the fun times, Grandma!' Feel sheepish.

4. (a) If you're a journalist, pitch a 2,000-word 'think piece' musing that Twitter represents everything wrong with society today. Include your killer line, 'TWITTER IS FOR TWITS'. Welcome a photographer into your home who takes pictures of you clutching your face and screaming to denote your frustration at the information age.

4. (b) Your column is retweeted around the Twitterverse. The general consensus is that you're 'an utter roaring flangehead'. You don't know about this – you're not on Twitter.

5. (a) Revisit Facebook. A stranger has requested you join their group 'I always leave the peach yoghurt in the multipack till last!' An ex-colleague, Rachel, has posted 77 photos of her newborn baby lying in the exact same position with an identical blank expression and added captions saying what she imagines the baby is thinking, such as 'Ooh mumsy I am so snuggly! More milky pwease!'

5. (b) Log off quickly as your Tourette's-style streak is compelling you to add the comment 'OH, GET A GRIP, RACHEL, FFS IT LOOKS LIKE A GIANT SLUG, LET'S BE HONEST.'

5. (c) Reject 87 Facebook event invites and a friend request from the boy at school who pretended Michael Jackson was his uncle. Admit to yourself that Facebook feels like having a part-time admin job at the National Institute of Ass-hats.

Entry level, stage one

1. Your Twitter resistance is crumbling. Every bloody time you try to share a nugget of gossip with a friend or a link to a blog or a YouTube clip, they say they saw it last week on Twitter. Oh, and they've been chatting with their favourite Hollywood film director about sub-plots.

And reading a new life-changing novel 'everyone's tweeting about'. They're becoming a pain in the arse. You can't beat them, you have to join them.

2. Secretly visit Twitter's homepage and read some of the scrolling 'top tweets'. They're mostly teen-angst garbage like this:

Teendream370 Sometimes, the only thing i want is to lock myself in my room, lay on the floor, listen to music and sob till i have no tears left. #OTQ

godsgirl8494 Never ignore a person who loves, cares & misses u cuz 1 day, u might wake up from ur sleep & realize u lost the moon while counting the stars.

Bieberbeliebergirl oh my god I just saw the new picture of justin on the front of WOW! mag and I cried so much I passed out!!!

Or American sports stars saying shit like this:

jonnoNYDN Knicks 3-3 since the trade! Denver 5-1? But that's not fair! Nuggets didn't have to play Cleveland twice.

And demented celebrities saying things a bit like:

TheRealTamaraBanana Me and my doggies walking on the beach in Malibu. Ooh sand in my tootsies!!!

3. Decide to join Twitter. If this is the intellectual level of a 'top tweet' you're going to be like the resident frickin' Stephen Hawking. You want IN.

Entry level, stage two

1. Click on the 'New To Twitter?' tab. Yes, you're a massive hypocrite after everything you've said. Rebrand this emotion as 'a willingness to learn and adapt'.

2. Choose a username. Everything vaguely resembling your name has been taken. Your number-one choice has been taken by a man in Tampa, Florida, who wears weightlifter vests and tweets about fancying Sarah Palin, squirrel-killing and running the Ice Road Truckers fan club. Decide not to challenge him for ownership.

3. Choose a password. Choose the same password you use for all of your other internet accounts, then write the password down on a neon-pink Post-it note and stick it somewhere obvious so the resident joker in your life has

full access to your Twitter account and can tweet your boss stuff like:

financeguru100 I am feeling sexual in my pee pee area wants sexy bareback funtimes?????

4. Become anxious about your blank Twitter profile page and the anonymous 'egg' symbol which represents you. Reflect sadly how the egg isn't a million miles away from your true body shape since you gave up Rumpblaster classes and discovered Eat.com Thai food deliveries.

5. Tackle your first 'What's happening?' box. Get ready for your first 'tweet'. All you need to say is what's happening. Fine. You can do this. No-one is asking you to herald a new art renaissance or design a new form of air travel. Just explain the status quo in your life.

6. Think for far too long about 'What's happening'. Nothing's bloody happening. Nothing at all. You're sat on the sofa staring at a laptop. You're a bit thirsty. The cat is scrunch-washing its arse. Who the hell wants to know this?

7. Type, 'I am on the sofa with a laptop on my knee.' Die a bit. Delete it.

8. In exasperation, finally type, 'DUNNO WOT I AM DOING HERE' in block capitals, then press tweet. Feel exposed and idiotic, like that time you fell asleep on the toilet after Cynthia's 25th and your friends Facebooked it. Fuck Facebook. Fuck the internet.

9. On Twitter's recommendation, decide to follow Stephen Fry. A tweet immediately shows up for him on your 'timeline' saying Stephen Fry is in Nairobi looking at a rare orchid and it is simply marvellous. Good for bloody Stephen. Stare at your greying knickers drying on a nearby radiator. Twitter isn't cheering you up.

10. Follow film star and celebrated beauty Liz Hurley. Liz says she's 'enjoying a delicious vodka tonic in front of a log fire post bikini shoot'. Stephen Fry is still looking at a rare orchid. You, the eggperson, simply 'DUNNO WOT I AM DOING HERE'.

11. EUREKA! Remember that your colleague Leona with the brave directional hairstyle and whistlestop social life has a TWITTER ADDRESS as part of her email signature. Type this address painstakingly into your web browser with your tongue dangling out of your mouth through concentration.

12. Stare in horror at Leona's Twitter page. She has 1,675

followers! How did she do that?? Her timeline is just a row of gibbering:

hahahLOLZ>> RT @katybun_s DID U SEEE HER??
http://bit.ly/lT6xtg (via @newman67) *6 minutes ago*

@parriah wot u chattin bout? *14 minutes ago*

@parriah Totes. Blates after her. Proper has the horn.
20 minutes ago

Thanks for all the #ffs! *1 hour ago*

@dangerlolz speak to @carlybunbuns about tix. *2 hours ago*

My FF's this week. Keeping me sane @tarquinbang @missyghost @toxicsue @godzilla1897 *3 hours ago*

13. Stare at the 'Follow' option on Leona's page. Feel like an enormous unpopular child lumbering into the sand-pit bellowing 'HALLO CAN I PLAY WITH YOU?' as Twitterdom dives under its mother's skirt for sanctuary.

14. Begin to completely overthink the word 'Follow'. It's rather menacing, isn't it? 'Hello, I'm FOLLOWING you,' you're whispering electronically. 'Don't be alarmed. I've decided to silently observe your life for my own per-

sonal gratification. Yes, up to this juncture, Leona, our friendship bond has only stretched to "moaning about pay" and "eating canteen macaroni cheese at the same table" but now I am watching your life remotely. Watching you "LOL" with your sister about buying tampons and you haranguing your boyfriend to clean up the sick in the spare room – and by the power of Greyskull, Leona, I am bloody loving it. Oh, Christ on a bike, it feels so wrong but at the same time so right. I'm an incorrigible nosy bastard and I will not, nay CAN NOT stop.' This is what you're saying. And you don't even care.

15. Become angry and frustrated with Twitter. Your timeline hasn't moved at all in an hour. None of your buddies Stephen Fry, Liz Hurley or Leona have even followed you back. No-one's sent you any tweets or messages. Of course, you wouldn't know if anybody was, as you don't know about the @mentions column or the direct-message box yet. Log off in a massive strop, declaring Twitter pointless. Neglect your page for an indeterminate period.

Mid-entry-level hiatus

1. Sit home alone listening to 'These Dreams' by Heart, hugging your knees and looking mournfully at the rain

battering your window, feeling that there's a big world out there and you're missing out.

2. Revisit Facebook. Your neighbour has invited you to join a slenderly veiled neo-Nazi subgroup called 'Join here if you think speakin English gud is somefink you need2do OK??' Shy away from shouting her down on this. She may indeed be a fascist but she's very efficient at taking in your Net-A-Porter shoe deliveries.

3. Mentally toy with the option of quitting the internet and all other modern communication and using only your traditional landline phone, which is currently under the sofa covered in cat hair and skin particles.

4. Oh, who are you kidding? The only people who call that landline these days are scammers claiming you've won a six-week sunshine cruise OR your mother screaming at you to turn the TV on RIGHT NOW as there's someone with a caravan which looks just like your Aunt June's caravan. Look! RIGHT NOW! Quick! Quick! Now! Turn it on now! Oh, you missed it.

Entry level, stage three

1. Return to Twitter. Discover your @mentions box and a string of messages from friends shouting, 'Woo-hoo! You're here!!'

2. Feel warm and fuzzy.

3. You've got FIFTEEN FOLLOWERS. How did that happen? Some of them you've never heard of. Reply to some people, without having a clue about privacy and who can read what. You just know it feels good.

4. You've been on Twitter over an hour now.

5. Be very brave. Decide to add a picture to your page. Take 86 different pictures of your face with your laptop webcam, pouting, sucking in your cheekbones and holding a hand up to cover your double chin.

6. Find one you can tolerate. Crop it, bleach the colour out, convert it to sepia. You look like a prostitute living in a ghost house.

7. Fill in your Twitter biography. Opt for three serious words and then a crazy wildcard joke, e.g. 'Zane Strang – Accountant, Father, Runner, MALE STRIPPER'. This shows you're a serious person, but with a solid streak of PARTY running in your blood.

8. Start to become enveloped by the soap opera of Twitter. People flirting and bickering, the timeline constantly evolving as they add links to blogs and start silly hashtags. You're putting jokes out there and getting back

ROFLs. On Twitter, people find you funny. Three hours have passed and you've not even moved to pee.

9. Your droll observation about *American Idol* gets retweeted several times. Your follower count jumps by 50. Experience your first Twitter head-rush. Vow to reach the 100 follower mark within 24 hours, even if it means begging people for RTs and calling in sick.

10. Receive your first direct message. Hang on a minute?! On Twitter you can have private conversations and you don't need to think in more than 140 characters? And you can pretty much stop replying at any juncture? This is social contact as you always dreamed of it! Hallelujah for Twitter!

Dependency stage

The first signs of Twitter addiction begin showing.

You spend hours sitting in one spot with a full bladder, reading jokes and commenting on pics. You have fully formed opinions on subjects you previously didn't give a crap about, like red-squirrel protection and who owns the Elgin Marbles. You're RTing rumours you've heard about a student sit-in in Soho and feeling like Che Guevara. You're flirting with totally inappropriate people on direct message and unfollowing people who've been tardy in following you back. You've fallen into a Twitter clique with its own in-jokes, hate-figures and sacred cows. You're obsessed with a particularly odious tweeter's timeline and can't stop looking at it. You have a Twitter client open in your web browser and another on your iPhone and you check it on the toilet, in meetings and at funerals. You know all the plants in your house need watering but today's hashtag game is #songsthatsoundlikepoo. You wake up in the morning and check Twitter before checking whether your kids have been stolen in the night by raiders. You use Twitter as a verb, noun and pronoun. 'I tweeted her.' 'It's in his tweet.' 'He's got himself into a tweet-war.' 'He's definitely twanking himself daft in the DM column.' You're preachy/vaguely intolerable on the subject of Twitter. You won't spare time for idiots who say Twitter is for twits because it makes you feel powerful, clever, funny, popular and the absolute opposite of how you feel in real life.

Welcome to Twitter.

Your next problem is that you can never, ever leave.

Justifying your Twitter addiction

Important things twits twaddle about

Once I'd made the jump from grumpy Twitter refusenik to full-blown believer, I was desperate to spread the word. But describing the joy of Twitter to non-users is verging on an insurmountable task. When faced with people sneering at you that Twitter is just egomaniacs broadcasting the details of their last wee, it's hard to persuade them otherwise with your sexy talk of 'real-time group-interface micro-blogging' or 'multi-user social-messaging platform'. This doesn't really nail that Twitter is about keeping in touch with lots of different, exciting, niche, real-time events all in one timeline. It doesn't describe how I might have spent the last hour following live courtroom tweets from the Old Bailey, while swapping jpegs of livid swans with your insomniac friend in Melbourne and trading snarky comments with the Westbro

Baptists circus show. And that was just from 10–11am. So, not just people posting pictures of their breakfast.

Here, to my mind, are Twitter's eight most vital uses:

1. Breaking news, aka: OMG! Look What Just Happened

In its purest form, Twitter thrives on breaking news – the constant techno sugar rush of millions of tweeters shouting what's happening right now. One of Twitter's strongest addictive properties is its inexhaustible supply of OMGs and WTFs racing up your timeline, giving you the heady air of an omniscient superbeing. Or a right old smart arse, anyway. Stuff like:

> 9.0 earthquake in Japan! My brother says his house is moving! *1 minute ago*
>
> Holy hell. There's a man with a bare arse fighting the polis on Sauchiehall Street! *8 minutes ago*
>
> Riot in Saint Germain. Ouch. Secret police truncheons making head very hurty. *10 minutes ago*

Twitter finally obliterated the notion that a 'trusted news source' is an established brand like Sky, CNN, BBC, etc. – an official reporter with great teeth and a roving mic delivering sage sound bites an hour after an event happened. Damn that. News is breaking on Twitter every minute of the day. Revolution, coup, riot, scandal, resignation, we hear it there first.

Crucially, anyone on Twitter can set themselves up as a trusted 'news filter' as long as they give good gossip and gain a reputation for getting the scoop and not grabbing the wrong end of the stick. Twitterdom rocks with earnest one-man box-bedroom Reuters units called stuff like @angryclaret909 and @torysnooperspy, who take breaking news very seriously and will quack on day and night about Westminster gossip, Premier League transfer hoohah, Middle Eastern splinter-cell terrorism and Hollywood film-set backstabbing, providing a sterling service to the world of 'news', yet never quite addressing today's equally pressing issues of 'paid work' or 'fresh underpants'.

To experience ultimate feelings of Godliness, I advise downloading a Twitter client such as TweetDeck or Echofon, then setting up multiple keyword columns for topics you want to monitor. Say, in my case: the *Guardian* newspaper, Tom Hardy, Hackney and, of course, Grace Dent. Now every mention of these topics being breathed into the Twitterverse – including my own name – is updating in real time on the computer perched on your lap. I'm monitoring the universe! Nothing gets past me. I'm Jack Bauer in *24*, I'm Q in Bond, I'm Tina Turner in *Beyond Thunderdome*. I'm Yoda in a plunge bra. I'm queen of the bloody world.

2. @gracedent is here

Twitter is ideal for letting friends keep track of your whereabouts:

> **gracedent** is in Claridge's Bar drinking espresso martinis

It couldn't be easier. Just update your 'What's happening?' box with the precise location of the bar, restaurant, club, park bench, etc., you're cluttering up, then, if you're lucky, your followers shall descend for an impromptu 'tweet-up'. Drinks will flow, LOLZ will ring out and everyone will go wild and forget their worries, just like in that Lionel Richie song 'All Night Long' (or was it 'Dancing on the Ceiling'? Let's face it, Lionel had a lot of crazy-ass nights out in the 80s – although not during his 'Hello' period. That blind chick seemed kind of serious. I digress . . .). What's certain is this: many work sickies have been chucked, marriages rocked, deadlines missed and toddlers left wobbly-lipped standing on nursery steps mumbling, 'Maybe mummy meant she come back on Friday' due to Twitter's lethal knack for co-ordinating 'people who want to party' with 'people who've already started drinking'.

Some people set geotagging map co-ordinates on their tweets, so you can flick to Google Maps and look at the street they live in or the restaurant where they're currently tackling the lobster thermidor. The best thing about Twitter geotagging is when the tweeter clearly doesn't know they've enabled the function and is evidently not where they claim to be. So the tweet says:

martinbigbossceo Another long night working on this pitch. Can't wait to get home.

Yet the co-ordinates say Martin's actually in Belgravia sat in a sushi restaurant, which is coincidentally where @cindyslagbag, the Australian temp who looks a lot like Jar Jar Binks but has a relaxed approach to thongs is tweeting from, too.

Personally, I'm quite guarded about stating my exact whereabouts. I tend to worry that posting something like this

suzieq One more Martini at Bar Bang, Hackney with @lizzierumba and @monica765. Already quite drunk.

has two sides to it. On one level, it shows everyone following @suzieq that she's having a fantastic night out (yeah, you heard, Glenda in corporate communications with your 'needing the group report distributed by 5pm' whining. It's Friday night and @suzieq is STEAMBOATS! Suck that!). On another level, it's an open invitation to @suzieq's mysterious follower @watcher57 – that tweeter with no avatar photo who only follows 3 people: @suzieq; a Missouri-based dominatrix called @empressasssmacker; and @officialMileyCyrus – to pop along and 'say hello'.

(Actually, come to think of it, @watcher57 probably wouldn't say hello to @suzieq. @watcher57 would just watch @suzieq silently from behind a plant near the cloakroom, and the fact @suzieq doesn't know would turn @watcher57 on.)

I also worry that tweeting my exact whereabouts is also extra-helpful for local burglars with usernames like @fivefingereddiscount and @pentonvillemike who want to break into your home, try on your pants and then scatter most of your DVDs along your driveway (because, let's face it, even burglars are judgemental about a person's decision to buy *Big Momma's House 2* on Blu-ray).[1] In most cases, however, the worst thing that will happen from tweeting something like

> **gracedent** watching Kylie at O2 arena is anyone here?

is that lots of really funny people join your group, you all carry on to an after-party, get hammered on tequila shots and damage your work-attendance record by calling in sick the next day.

3. Look who I'm with!!

Although a lot of tweeters won't say exactly where they are, most of them can't resist shouting about WHO they're hanging out with. Cue acres and acres of this:

---

1 Obviously, these are worst-case examples of what might happen from tweeting your whereabouts. I apologise for my grave and scaremongering tone here, which I put down to a childhood living in a house where the *Daily Mail* was the sole newspaper. This bred in me the morbid certainty that everything which might go wrong probably will, from 'swans' (volatile neck-breakers) to 'talking to French people' (nation of rapists) and, obviously, eating badly cooked kidney beans (fatally poisonous).

josiedrivel Wonderful glam dinner with @susiecamel and @binkieboo. The gossip is FLOWING.

susiecamel So happy it's Friday. Such a hard week.

Martinamooch quiet Friday night in. Think dog has fleas again.

binkieboo Already one bottle of bubbles down. @susiecamel and @josiedrivel being the nadir of hilarity.

josiedrivel I wish @susiecamel would stop flirting with the waiter!!!

All very jolly or annoying or both at the same time. Twitter is voyeur heaven. If I follow everyone in your clique, you might not know me, but I'm at perfect liberty to watch your entire social life unfolding, tweet upon tweet. I can watch you like a real-life soap opera. I know where you're going tonight. I know who's having dinner with you. I know who didn't get invited and is sending wounded little tweets about it. I know who's more excited about your night out than anyone else and who never really had any intention of showing up. I can see that @susiecamel told a white lie to a different circle of friends about what she was doing and now @josiedrivel has grassed her up.[2]

By the sheer amount of info available, plus the ability to search usernames and to search back through conversations, Twitter allows total strangers to form intimate bonds – by proxy – with your clique. They can follow the shifting hierarchies and unfolding power plays. They can gossip on DM with other cliques about the spiralling outer cogs and pretenders to your clique's throne. Yes, I am still talking about someone in a Slanket sitting on a sofa watching 'folk arranging to eat at Pizza Express'. The good thing about watching someone else's clique is that it reassures you exactly how brilliant/funny/well-adjusted your clique is. It rarely occurs to you that people think the same about your Twitter clique. (For a full range of reasons 'Why Your Twitter Clique Is Better Than Their Clique', please go to the appended cut-out-and-keep Twitter *Clique versus clique* checklist.)

Viewing the unfolding social map of your friends, family

---

2   This won't have crossed the mind of @josiedrivel when she posted that she was off out with @susiecamel. @josiedrivel is utterly blinded by the sugar-rush of letting strangers know she's out having fun with @susiecamel because @susiecamel reads the travel news on BBC Radio Weybridge and is a little bit famous, which improves @josiedrivel's standing in Twitterdom.

and acquaintances from your omniscient cyber-view-point is fantastic. It feels like being God. Actually, now I think about it, being on Twitter is better than being God because, let's be frank, vast swathes of Earth's inhabitants aren't even sure God exists, but EVERYONE knows for certain Twitter exists. I'll go out on a limb here and say if Twitter and God went up against each other in a Top Trumps game, Twitter would kick God's ass.[3]

Of course, according to your state of mind (and, as I think I've proved over the course of the past pages, mine is totally tip top), watching an entire evening of @josiedrivel, @susiecamel and @binkieboo planning a 'fabby night out' can be:

(a) Riveting, funny, feelgood. What will happen next? Do they realise anyone is watching this? Do they realise that wasn't a direct message, that it was in the timeline? Oh this is brilliant, fetch the popcorn. Or:

(b) Massively irritating. In fact, just like being whisked back to puberty and hearing all the cool kids discussing

3 Note to self: check if claiming an anthropomorphised Twitter is 'better than God' and could properly beat his head in during a fight might cause tension with fundamentalist religious groups. Sure it will be fine. Actually, just go with it.

tonight's amazing party to which you're not invited as you have a beard of acne and recurrent sties.

If you're feeling more like (b), it is advisable to turn off your laptop and do something else. No good can come of being on Twitter in this state of mind and you are at dire risk of entering 'The desktop multi-application manual-refresh spiralling circle of hell' (see *What is desktop multi-application spriralling circle of hell syndrome?*, Appendix II).

Of course, celebrities, their entourages and their hangers-on are totally addicted to playing 'Look Who I'm With'. You'll be forgiven for thinking some people on Twitter build their entire career out of being a plus-one to someone with talent, and the Twitter timeline is the perfect place to ram this home day after day. As a rule of thumb, the more desperate the individual to be further up the showbiz pecking order, the more toe-curling their bragging is about who's around their table on Saturday night 'enjoying a delicious tagine! Three bottles of bubbles down already!'

Marthaprguru Can't believe I'm late for my mohito with Kylie.

Donnyhairtothestars lovely poolparty! Matt le blanc's kids are sooooo scrumptious.

Lizzielocket Love the Beckhams. Vicky makes a mean Thai curry!!!

Obviously, it could be levelled that if these people were spending time with genuine friends that they actually cared a jot about, they'd log off Twitter, interact with them and stop using famous people to boost their own personal 'brand'. Perhaps, in the wake of Twitter, the classiest thing a person can do if they spend time with another person is switch off their phone and never breathe a word about it. This would be noble, yes, but would make Twitter very dull. Come ye bigheads, namedroppers and starfuckers, one and all. We LOVE you.

Appendix I

Your clique versus their clique

Your clique is hilarious, the voice of a generation. Their clique is full of unfunny wankers

Your clique is sassy and snarky. They are bitter, one-note bitches.

Your clique is witty. They are prone to sickening whimsy.

Your clique is tongue-in-cheek and self-deprecating. Their clique is just a bunch of mediocre self-congratulatory dicks.

Your clique is on Twitter all day hanging out as it's a good way of staying up to date. Their clique is on Twitter all day because they've got nothing else going on in their sad lives.

Your clique is really quite humble. They think they're fucking it.

Your clique rarely mentions its good fortune. They bang on all day about their achievements and, like, who fucking cares?

Your clique is totally confident in who it is and is copying nobody. They wish they were your clique. It's so obvious. They even copy your words and phrases and in-jokes.

You would never want to be in their clique. Their clique would give their right arm to be in your clique.

Your clique saw their clique on Twitter at like fucking 3am. Your clique only noticed as they checked Twitter on the way back from a party. Their clique had never even been out.

Your clique always checks to see if their clique is going to something. If their clique has been invited, it's obvious they've invited bloody anyone.

Your clique and their clique are as bad as each bloody other. All the other cliques can see this.

Appendix II

What is desktop multi-application spiralling circle of hell syndrome?

General information: 'Desktop multi-application spiralling circle of hell syndrome' is a zombie-like, depressed state reached during 'leisure time' spent staring at a computer screen with many different applications and numerous web pages open at once, over a prolonged period.

The victim's concentration span declines to 20-second bursts, and the pointer on their mouse roams listlessly, without aim, around and around the desktop, clicking on applications (for example: Twitter, email, iChat, Safari, Spotify, iCal), never quite dealing with anything and moving on.

A typical spiral might see the victim skim-reading news pages, clicking on blog links, editing email boxes, refreshing message-board chats, typing Twitter responses, servicing a Skype chat, before repeating the pattern, over and over again, with a growing state of anxiety about life. Standing up and leaving the computer screen becomes not only impossible but futile, as 'in the spiral' the real world seems a very hectic and scary place.

This syndrome is abundant in home-workers, freelancers, students and any other profession with a blurred concept of work time and leisure time. Although the spiral occurs in 'leisure time', it has no restorative or relaxing properties, despite the victim vehemently claiming that it does.

During an attack, the victim might look up from his/her screen, one hand clamped over their flickering migraine-stricken eye, resembling a toddler imitating a pirate, and grunt, 'No, I'm fine, I don't need fresh air. I'm doing THIS!' On being questioned as to what they are actually 'doing', the victim will find this almost impossible to clarify.

A typical multi-application spiralling circle of hell contains all of these applications:

The email inbox

The victim's email inbox will contain 90 or more opened

but undealt-with emails sporting head-bangingly dull subject headings like 'Source notes for grant-funding presentation: READ asap' or 'Amendments to lobby drain project for sign off'. One of the emails is typically a 15-part epic production, CCing everyone in the entire office, running the gamut of everyone's thoughts, counter-thoughts and contradictions. The point of this CC chain would take at least an hour for the victim to unravel, resulting in the victim realising the problem never involved them in the first place. The inbox also contains emails full of passive-aggressive snark from neglected family members, emails from friends including photos of their children which need to be tactfully commented on, and RSVP requests for birthdays and social occasions (which the victim will stare at mournfully as this task involves liaising calendars with their partner, booking hotels and letting down other people whom they've double-booked, which will require writing even more difficult emails).

During the spiral the victim will keep returning to the email inbox panel, pruning off spam Viagra offers, Facebook friend-request notifications and Twitter-follower updates like a Bonsai gardener without actually tackling the rambling ivy of undealt-with 'work', because the victim is, as they keep insisting, 'NOT at work'.

Safari/Firefox/Chrome/Explorer

The victim may have eight or more web-browser screens open, which might include:

(i) A live TV channel (iPlayer/TVCatchup) with audible volume.

(ii) An internet forum messageboard thread about a hobby (football, music, TV, role-playing) where a crowd of indigenous forum posters are making gossipy small-talk. The victim has been visiting this board for years and will lurk silently reading the threads, hating everyone there but finding their bitterness compelling and a good benchmark of everything he or she hopes they're not.

(iii) An online newspaper site such as the *Guardian/Times/New York Times*. The victim is skim-reading serious breaking news about worrying events in the Middle East and other bloody foreign conflicts, but has also entered into an futile argument in the comments thread of an arts feature leading to a tit-for-tat argument with someone in another house suffering from desktop multi-application spiralling circle of hell syndrome. Computer programmers are working on software so families of people suffering from this syndrome can locate and direct-message each other to make arrangements to socialise together, leaving their two idiot internet warriors bashing each other with cyber-clubs.

(iv) A corporate or work-related website where the victim can skim reports about the dire state of their industry, and look at recent job reallocations, promotions and pay structuring. The site will feature many pictures of colleagues who are far more skilful networkers laughing and drinking with senior board members at social events, at which the victim can stare and fume.

(v) A badly written blog by an amateur writer which has yet to suggest its intention 700 words in. It was arrived at via a travel diary clicked on half-heartedly while the victim was trying to prune off emails. The blog documents every Bacon McMuffin and look-out-of-the-window which has happened between Gatwick South and Caracas and rambles on for 5,000 words lacking any moment of real sparkle, like Phileas Fogg on Xanax.

(vi) A comedy meme site full of photo galleries that aren't even very funny but led the victim to click through hundreds of pictures of Dogs That Look Like Lenin and send links out to Twitter buddies which they are now anxious no-one found funny.

(vii) Remnants of an internet porn foray which didn't get closed down properly, and every time they do try to close it the browser unleashes another page of willies and front bottoms which look frankly vile in this light, now they've long since served their purpose.

Other miscellaneous pages include: at least five Wikipedia pages; a paused YouTube clip which wouldn't stream properly; a half-completed Tesco.com order abandoned because the victim can't be bothered to walk to the kitchen and check what they actually need; several online shopping pages of coats and jackets from Asos.com, Net-A-Porter.com or OiPolloi.com that the victim can't really afford but has added to an imaginary basket anyway; an online fantasy football league game they've lost interest in playing; some TripAdvisor.com reports casing out a holiday featuring reviews from American holidaymakers furious that it took six minutes to check in to their luxury resort hotel, and to add insult to injury their favourite soda water was not available behind the infinity-pool bar.

Skype/iChat

The victim has opened one or more instant-messaging applications with the purpose of chatting to a friend in real time about a specific subject. The conversation has since run dry, yet both sides have left the application open and are now commenting sporadically on things they're watching on TV, at the same time as debating the various meta-stories they can see playing out on Twitter.

Additionally, the spiral victim is receiving incoming chats and face-to-face requests from other friends, which they are ignoring – these intrusions make them feel very put upon. Often the victim sets their Skype/iChat/AIM position to 'permanently invisible', but then forgets they've done so and becomes anxious and paranoid about friends/family/unrequited-loves who appear on-line as 'available' but aren't starting conversations with them.

Spotify/iTunes/other music player

At some point in the spiral, the victim begins looking on-line for a track that they can't quite remember the name of, but they do know a few words of the chorus, which is no bloody help whatsoever as those words are 'oooh loving you . . . ooo shoo be doo'. The victim will randomly return to this application and trawl through dozens of potential songs. If they do find the song they are looking for, they will then trawl through dozens of disco club re-mixes and 2010 reimaginings, never quite hitting on the exact feel and sound they wanted. Finding this song has become imperative as it will sound really great when the victim is 'out jogging'. Ironic, as the victim rarely leaves the house.

Photo album

The victim is grabbing photos sent to them as email attachments and transferring them to their album. They don't approve of the way they look in any of these photos so they are cropping, trimming and bleaching the shots and then adding to a photo album they never ever look at. Each time the victim looks at their photo-album application, a mild anxiety grips them that:

(a) they might lose all the photos as they're not backed up; and

(b) they should be behaving as amazingly as those families in online Apple Mac seminars and sharing the photos, or turning them into a multimedia presentation, or linking them up on three-way videochat with people of many different ethnicities all over the world, or weaving the pictures into a stock-templated newsletter and sending it to everyone with a backing score of 'Fast Car', by Tracy Chapman, played on a piccolo.

Twitter

The victim has TweetDeck, Echofon or AN Other Twitter application open on their laptop screen, but is also occasionally visiting the web version, www.Twitter.com, as they don't have 100% confidence in their application when it comes to deleting tweets, reporting accurate RT scores or even updating their timeline quickly enough. Multiple storylines are happening all at once on their Twitter timeline – none of which are of much interest but which are cluttering a vast section of the brain: e.g. the closure of a library in Dorset (please RT), someone whining that they've discontinued their favourite NARS lipstick, two tweeters flirting with each other by sending back and forth hair-pulling, and 'oh look I am throwing your satchel in the school pond' cyber strutting.

The victim is concurrently sickened by their transparency and depressed that no-one is flirting with them. The victim is monitoring their own Twitter clique and is occasionally adding to conversations but has nothing particularly fresh or lively to say as they've been cooped up in one spot for far too long with a dry mouth and haven't eaten hot food for 24 hours. The victim has become engrossed yet again in the goings-on of a rival clique and is watching them preparing for a night out. The victim is harbouring all sorts of crossness and resentment for the rival clique for their showiness and bragging, and has taken to bitching about the rival clique on direct message with members of their own clique.

Despite the victim being, on a day-to-day basis, totally intolerable on the subject of Twitter, claiming it makes them feel more powerful, clever, funny and popular, right at this moment it makes them feel as cheery as a Leonard Cohen unplugged session in the waiting room of a Swiss suicide clinic.

Treatment for desktop multi-application spiralling circle of hell syndrome

Warning: Once entered, the spiral of doom is difficult to snap out of without assertive and volatile direct action.

This might include:

(i) Grabbing the laptop out of the victim's sweaty hands and throwing it in a koi carp pond.

(ii) Threatening to divorce/break up with the victim, accompanied by an elaborate playacting session of packing a Samsonite suitcase with underwear and socks and screaming, 'You never change. You say you will, but you never do. I'm leaving. Find another fucking wife/girlfriend/husband, etc., on TWITTER!'

(iii) Smashing internet router into small digestible pieces with a meat-tenderising hammer, then baking it into a quiche.

(iv) Taking kitchen scissors out of drawer and lopping off lumps of your own hair, shouting, 'MALCOLM! NOTICE ME! I AM YOUR WIFE FOR FUCK'S SAKE! Stop arguing with those dickheads on the *Guardian* Comment Is Free site and let's go out to the pub!'

(v) Beginning a new relationship and bringing the shag-ee home to have loud sex with them in the spare room, stopping midway to post a picture online, adding the @ username of the spiral victim with the message 'ANY CHANCE OF AN RT FOR THIS?'

Long-term outlook

Bleak. Medical research for this syndrome is in its infancy, so please, please send any money to www.justbegging.com/anothercharitytweetyesiwillhave-theshirtoffyourbackthatlldonicely.

Do dig deep for this worthy cause.

4. Tweet-a-long television

Welcome to the world's biggest sofa.

On Twitter you'll find millions of TV addicts – who, just like you, should really be filing their VAT return or wallpapering the landing – all tweeting along to the same programme. On Twitter, we're one large, dysfunctional, square-eyed, snarky family. Our laptops perch on our plump pot bellies as we go bitching and LOLing at a plethora of TV trash.

We find unity in derision at the Black Eyed Peas at half-time in the Super Bowl or Pope Benedict XVI's visit to London or the frothy idiocy of Saturday night's *Strictly Come Dancing* dance-off. The dafter, more soul-zapping the show is, the funnier Twitter becomes.

Just say a harrowing docudrama pops up on Channel 4 called *Me and My Wind: A Life Marred by Flatulence*, you can bet your ass that Twitter will come alive, with 1% of your timeline hoping to discuss the harrowing plight of irritable bowel syndrome and the other 99% hoping for a fart-based hashtag game to brighten up their night.

Winds of Change #fartmusic

Beyond Thunderdome #fartmusic

Another One Bites the Dust by Queen #fartmusic

Up the Junction by The Squeeze (the cheese) #fartmusic

I find Twitter comforting. It makes me feel less lonely in my bamboozlement at Planet Earth. I can see 600 million children squealing about Justin Bieber and his powerful, all-consuming charisma at the MTV Awards and I can tweet stuff like this:

> OMG has creepy popbot 3.0 Justin Bieber ruptured his perineum or does he just dance like that? #mtvawards

And, sweet lord, people RT it and LOL and even ROFL ... and I am healed.

Or during Michael Jackson's memorial service, when sane-minded individuals the world over gathered to tweet 'SERIOUSLY MAN, WTF?' as Usher pirouetted beside the casket and the 12-year-old runner-up of *Britain's Got Talent* was drafted in to sing 'Who's Loving You?'

> **CharlesinCharge** There is a young boy singing a love song to Michael Jackson's casket. Oh. Now that's AWKWARD.

You're not alone. People are noticing the strange shit you're noticing. And what's more, Twitter shafted that adland concept of 'the watercooler moment', e.g. waiting until tomorrow morning in the vain hope that Glenda saw the same thing as you. Screw Glenda! Screw all those nimrods at work with their 'Actually I don't have a telly' chat. You've got Twitter now. In fact, warn people not to bother approaching you about pop culture at all unless their chat is as good as this:

sourpuss18 Why does Helena Bonham Carter bother paying a stylist? She looks like a sexually assaulted Hawthorn bush. #BAFTA *2 minutes ago*

guantanamomike Oh I see Madonna been on that magic horse which keeps licking all the old off her again. *4 minutes ago*

baglady1000 Damn, it's the episode of Eastenders where everyones acts clinically depressed and Phil chins someone. I've seen this one. #eastenders *6 minutes ago*

OMG you killed Twitter, you bastard

I love how Twitter unites the world in such fervent LOLs the entire system actually breaks, leaving the screen filled with that dreaded aquatic tosspot the 'Fail Whale' (see *Who is the Fail Whale?* below). Take, for example, the moment when close-harmony indie-folk tormentors Mumford & Sons took to the stage at the 2011 British MTV Awards clad in cowboy hats and snazzy waistcoats, hands clasped to their ears, to deliver a rousing a cappella ... only for Twitter to implode with SHEER IRE.

ClarkyCat These were the fuckers who stole my dad's combined harvester.

bizzimbean Mumford are the sort of tossers who camp beside you at Glastonbury forcing you to retreat into hard research chemicals and special brew.

GillyGirl2 OI MUMFORD. There was a reason they cancelled Dukes of Hazzard.

Giving way to:

Instantdonkey FUCK. Keep getting Fail Whale. Mumford broke Twitter. #fuckmumford

Boring Q: But doesn't wasting a lot of time watching TV while being on Twitter make people lazy and slothful?

A: No. Utter balderdash. Tweeters are highly ambidextrous types. We're watching telly while simultaneously monitoring our timelines and @ mentions and flirting secretly on direct-message, fighting flamewars, winning a hashtag game and all the while tracking delivery of Cantonese Set Meal C. Future tweeting generations will most likely evolve bug eyes which spin like Las Vegas fruit machines and look super-beautiful in volume-enhancing mascara. We will look awesome.

Trust me, I'm a critic

Twitter transformed my work as a TV critic. Suddenly, I could get a stark snapshot, in real time, of what TV fans all over the world are getting excited about. Foreign TV that was still in post-production, stuff no British TV channel had thought of acquiring yet. Things that would never play in Britain anyway, but for which kind tweeters would sort out hush-hush viewings. I heard very early on about TV like HBO's *True Blood* and AMCs *Breaking Bad*. Scottish TV like *Limmy's Show*, *Burnistoun* and *The Scheme*, Danish drama *The Killing* and French police show *Spiral*. Now, I can sit in east London reading on-the-sofa reports of hidden TV gems, before snooping about for preview tapes. In the days pre-Twitter I was at the full mercy of entertainment public-relations departments, their schedules, politics and agenda. This, quite honestly, made getting hold of footage of TV shows as pleasurable as a long bout of banging my head against an Artexed support wall. I would write something like this:

Dear Jocasta, head of publicity for Bang!TV

I have heard your TV station has just spent a million pounds on Killer Truck Karnage and I would like see it, please, if that's OK with you, with a view to making a big noise about it and getting viewers excited.

Yours, Grent xx

Only to be greeted with one of the following:

(a) Solid fucking silence.

(b) A noncommittal airy-fairy reply saying they've only just bought the show and it's not on the transmission schedule yet, so maybe I should mail back in about four months' time.

(c) Just go away altogether.

(d) Don't speak to me, this isn't really me, speak to Annabella, oh, Annabella has gone on maternity – no, speak to Zane. Oh, Zane has never heard of it [communication terminated].

Nowadays, I can tweet this:

gracedent Anyone seen ep 1 Killer Truck Karnage?

And, lo! Somewhere in the Twittersphere there's a *Killer Truck Karnage* fan with KILLER TRUCK KARNAGE set up as keywords on a list in his TweetDeck application who will lure me with a:

Karnster3 Pssst, send me a DM.

And then:

Here's link where ep 1 KTK is. If that doesn't work I can burn you a copy.

This was a GAMECHANGER. I do giggle down my sleeve sometimes when I hear PRs claiming to have launched a wonderful 'whisper campaign' on some big mega-bucks TV acquisition, when in actual fact Twitter, where real-life TV addicts can make noise in 140 characters, was where the buzz started. In fact, the only 'whisper' I heard from the PR was when I requested preview footage and their 'Out of Office' reply told me to buzz off as they were at the Cannes Festival.

A load of balls

But for pure feelgood vibes, I love hanging about Twitter in the wee small hours when there's cricket on TV live from India or Australia and my timeline transforms into a night-shift of gentle menfolk gently discussing googlies, stumps and bouncers. Obviously, I haven't got the remotest idea how cricket works but this doesn't spoil my enjoyment. To my comprehension, cricket is simply a lot of men in heavy SPF nose-block titting about in white knitwear, while a number of other men stand in the bar at the side of the pitch waving at them while eating pork pies. This can go on for any time upwards of 22 hours. Still, I do love the gentle nocturnal burble of cricket-tweets. It's 3am and all feels well.

Appendix III

Who is the Fail Whale?

Benign aquatic bloater. Smug sea-faring git. Fun-prohib-iting flubber. Watery wanker. Impassive, benign, moon-faced idiot. Improbably carried, impudent, inky bloater.

Moby Dickhead. Blubbery harbinger of impotent rage. Dreadful aquatic tosspot. Etc. Nobody likes you, Fail Whale. We don't care whether you're specially designed to bring a snuggly touchy-feely moment to a frustrating techno-crisis. Look at you, with your mung-bean-munching, hippy smile. Your 'Hey, chill, man, don't worry about it' expression does not seem to honour the fact that I have a very, very hilarious one-liner about the volume of the shadow chancellor's hair on *Question Time* that I need to blast out into the cosmos (gaining moderate titters from a small audience and no reaction at all from the majority), but I am addicted to the thrill and by the time you get your act together the moment will have passed. You stupid, krill-sucking cockhead. Jesus Christ, Bill Hicks could appear from heaven for 20 minutes only, float angelically towards Twitter hoping to post a new set of material he'd been working on which would unite the planet in satirical glee, and you, fucking Fail Whale, would be there hovering about surrounded by your dismal orange dove disciples, being all, 'Hey, Bill, doood, I don't think Twitter is working, man, yeah, I don't know what's gone wrong with the system – here, have an ice-pop, let's just kick back and listen to some John Cougar Mellencamp, oh shit, Bill Hicks is gone . . .' I hate you, Fail Whale, you Zen-like, techno-taunting Japanese lunch buffet.

5. Twitter people love to help

Q: Do we, in accordance with popular moan, live in a cruel, self-serving world where your average man in the street would rather stab you than do anything nice for you?

A: NO. Don't be a berk.

Twitter time and time again proves this premise to be 'bollocks'. The Twittersphere reverberates with mega-helpful, downright lovely people who want to help you out. Lost cat? Need to borrow bagpipes? Feel like punching the shit out of your bigot sister-in-law at Christmas dinner? Ask Twitter for help. Your timeline will bubble with this type of wisdom:

> **gracedent** Do any of your neighbours' kids have a Princess Castle in the garden? My cat was locked in one for three days.

> **gracedent** Got bagpipes in my loft. Asshole ex-husband left them. I'm in Missouri, you're in East London. Any use? Fedex?

> **gracedent** You need to punch your sister-in-law somewhere on the torso then your mum won't see the bruises.

Twitter is full of sagacious, giving types offering their wisdom up to the electronic cosmos. This makes it fantastic for gleaning instant local info. Tweeters are the sort of folk who, if you asked for directions, would not only try to help, they'd walk you TO the location while sharing a tube of Smarties. Try tweeting:

I'm in Wolverhampton and STARVING.

Not only will people shout names of exemplary kebab shops and tea rooms at you, one person with a slender grasp of the idea of 'social boundaries' will doubtless insist you proceed straight to their own mother's house, ring the doorbell and ask her to cook her legendary shepherd's pie. Twitter is the saviour of tourists, as its inhabitants are everyday punters speaking from harsh experience. Twitter doesn't want you to spend your bank holiday in a queue for a dismal waxworks museum staring drably at 'Arnold Schwarzenegger', who is essentially a gigantic melted altar candle in a joke-shop wig.

Just a girl, looking at a screen, asking it to help her

Personally, I find Twitter extra-useful for answering the

womanly grooming befuddlements that I never quite see covered in glossy magazines. For example:

gracedent Why does every dark red lipstick I buy make me look like Ronald Macdonald once I put it on at home?

gracedent There is a spot under my eyebrow which feels like a brushed aluminium ball-bearing. Am I turning into a unicorn?

gracedent Why do I always look like Max Wall in leggings? Or at best like I'm wearing stay-puffed jodhpurs. WHY?

In these cases the collective ken of Twitter advised I should experiment with the lipsticks mid-afternoon in Asda or Tesco. Then I can smear one on and faff about in the frozen foods until the lipstick shade has revealed its true identity under the harsh strip lights. Genius. With regards to my ball-bearing spot, there was some online debate over whether the spot was a brain tumour or merely the beginnings of a second, even more evil-looking face. (Eventually, it turned out to be just a really big spot, but it was a comfort that I had many thirtysomething female followers around the world dealing with similar skin eruptions that made them resemble the cast of *Star Trek: Deep Space Nine*.) Sadly no-one knew how to make me look good in leggings, but plenty of male tweeters with usernames like @hardhumper and @billypython offered, very kindly, to come round to my house and drink wine until I was less concerned about wearing any.

The TwIT crowd

For instant, free IT help there's really no better place to hang out than Twitter, the home of a million computer addicts with usernames like @macmuncher and @gigobitegraham who are powerless to stop themselves helping you locate lost files, sync your Macs or bitchslap that router into compliance.

> **gracedent** What has happened to the sound on YouTube? Is my mac broken!?
>
> **gigobitegraham** have you muted it?
>
> **gracedent** Oh. Yes. Thanks dude.

Obviously, if you're a Mac user, you may have to endure a little pre-assistance whining about your decision to buy an Apple product when you could have bought a much uglier, joyless, sludge-coloured product which didn't sync with anything for MUCH LESS MONEY, but, hey, just bite your lip and keep smiling. There's much talk on Twitter about the divide between the famouses and the non-famouses, and more of this later, but in the meantime I must say how gratifying I find it that A-list celebs may possess defined cheekbones, perky buns and whopping bank balances but are utterly screwed as to how to attach a Word document to an email in Outlook Express without a man called @bogieeatingboris from Doncaster spoonfeeding instructions to them.

TheRealTamaraBanana omg! My blog has disappeared. All my thoughts about Malibu and scientology! I am devastated!

bogieeatingboris Don't worry. I bet I can find it. Have you looked in your hard drive's documents file?

TheRealTamaraBanana OH BORIS YOU'RE SUCH A STAR!

Outside of Twitter, Tamara Banana pays a 300lb man called @Meatboulder to stop people like Boris approaching her. On Twitter she is rolling over like a kitten to have her celebrity belly tickled.

Helper beware

Obviously, in the asking-for-help stakes, some people just take the piss. I have a particularly low tolerance for the plethora of 'RT my blog about self-harming/rabbit torture/my moans about the suggested B47 bypass' tweets. I'm even less patient about blatant 'Do My Job For Me' tweets, mainly by journalists and writers:

Authorgirlphyllis Has anyone got any great first-hand anecdotes about disastrous first dates?

gracedent No. Why don't you try imagining some with your brain seeing as you're supposed to be an author. #lazycow

Or the one that boils my piss:

Showbizsam Off to interview Madonna [or insert any celeb name]. Anything you want me to ask them!??

gracedent No, I'd like you to stop basically bragging about your schedule while disclosing you don't have an original thought in your head.

Media types are the worst offenders for taking advantage of Twitter's goodwill. Utter chancers. I have watched in complete awe as freelance women's mag writers with names like @josiedrivel have reached 3,000 followers chiefly via their anodyne twaddle about nail varnish, and sunk into a full-blown '3,000 follower syndrome' melt-down, supposing themselves the new Norah Ephron and firing out tweets like this:

josiedrivel Need intern to source original stories, transcribe interviews and do admin in return for a great reference.

gracedent While you do what, Josie? Fart about on Twitter playing hashtag #beatlesporn? JOG ON.

@gracedent's advice kiosk

Dear @gracedent

I've heard talk of a quite ghastly condition called 3,000 follower syndrome and believe my Twitter friend may be showing symptoms of it.

She now has 3,378 followers and has started to become rather starry, is convinced people recognise her 'off Twitter' in the street (they don't) and that she is best friends with a number of TV presenters whom she's spoken to online. Can you tell me what other symptoms to look out for?

Yours, @endofmytether

Dear @endofmytether

Poor you. You were completely correct to approach me on this matter. This '3,000 follower syndrome' happens to many perfectly pleasant tweeters as they head towards the 3,000-follower mark. Much like a Gremlin fed cream buns after midnight, the soft fluffy outer casing of the once quite normal tweeter is shed to reveal the incorrigible Twitter monster.

The typical sufferer:

– Was a sweet, affable character at 300, 400, 800 and 1,000-plus followers.

– Becomes gradually more obstreperous and verbose around the 2,500 mark.

– Around 3,000+ followers starts to think of themselves as something of a Twitter lynchpin.

– Worries that they are being recognised in the street. Finds this 'infringement of their privacy' a bit of a pain in the ass.

– Keeps drawing people's attention to the fact they are on Follow Friday lists with Stephen Fry, Sarah Silverman, etc., saying, 'Such fine company! I am sooo not worthy!'

– Begins to dismiss people they were previously friends with as 'stalkers'.

– Has picked up some celebrity followers whom they ruthlessly cyber-rim all day long, enquiring after their kids, trying to solve their problems and other obsequious methods of general inveiglement.

– Begins to believe there is a definite divide between 'us' (fabulous important tweeters) and 'them' (muggles).

– Begins to RT praise about their Twitter feed as a bastion of knowledge, gossip, comedy or breaking news.

– Begins to RT praise and @ in their employer's Twitter or anyone they might want a job with in the future.

– Begins to run competitions from their Twitter and offers up their possessions as competition prizes.

– Begins running 'teaser campaigns' from their Twitter timeline promising they will reveal something about themselves in return for more followers.

– Apologises in advance to fans that they might not be able to tweet in certain circumstances, e.g. a funeral or during their sister's home birth, but will try their best so as not to disappoint.

– Group-thanks people for Follow Fridays as they have been so 'swamped'.

– Group-responds to the question that apparently 'everyone' is asking them. If you check their feed, nobody is actually speaking to them.

– Resorts to more and more desperate tactics to get a rise out of Twitter. (Talking endlessly about their vagina or penis; naming whom they have or haven't had sex with or whom they would like to have sex with; appearing on Twitter drunk.)

– Has changed their Twitter bio to a job title which isn't actually true, e.g. 'award-winning PR' (their company won an award in 2006), 'author' (has failed to get a book deal), multimedia webscaper (can roughly use Photoshop), digital strategist (is only person in company who understands Twitter).

– Has been called into their boss's office at least once and asked to cut down their tweeting.

– Has unofficially and without permission begun seeing self as the Twitter face of the company.

– Has already got into trouble with staff members for giving answers on behalf of the company on Twitter.

– Is deeply wounded if anyone disagrees with them on
Twitter and begins firing out tweet after tweet making
their holier-than-thou position clear lest it ruin their Twitter 'brand'.

– Is getting a name as one-man/woman twitchfork mob.

– Gets into arguments with people and then begins putting
a full stop in front of @ replies to the person so that
everyone can keep track of this highly important feud.

– Sets up a page on Facebook to run concurrently with
Twitter where they can post more detailed info about
their thoughts/feelings or whims for their 'fans'.

– Has noticed that former friends/followers no longer
speak to them but think this is because they are jealous
of their success.

I'm not going to lie to you @endofmytether, the prog-
nosis with this condition is not very positive. I sometimes
find an extended period of shouting, 'Bitch, you ain't all
that!' and some good old-fashioned round-house slap-
ping will shock a sufferer back to their normal state,
but in many cases symptoms will only augment and the
only thing to do is to UNFOLLOW. This may very well

lead to you receiving the highly awkward 'oh why have you unfollowed-me email of doom'. On a happier note, you can always make nice new non-idiot friends who just want to shoot the breeze with no ulterior motives. There's millions of them on Twitter.

Love, @gracedent

6. Word-of-mouth buzz

The brevity of 140 characters makes Twitter the perfect place to broadcast sincere joy. To shout out that delicious, all-consuming heartfelt glee one fizzes with while reading an amazing chapter in a novel. Or walking out of a cinema wanting to grab passers-by, point up at the Now Showing sign and yell: 'THAT WAS REALLY GOOD!'

> **calmpanda** Been up till 3am with Rose Tremaine Music and Silence. How did I miss this?
>
> **BiscuitBoy** Crap week but OMG 'Hot Rod' with Danny McBride made me do a little LOL puddle in my pants. It's on amazon for £3!

Sod going home and slaving over a blog entry. In fact,

post-Twitter my guilt over whether I needed a blog at all was pleasantly assuaged. Obviously, some blogs are pinnacles of literary splendour, their owners highly disciplined, their pages constantly tweaked and updated. On the other hand, my experience of blogging was:

(a) feeling guilty about not blogging and feeling jealous of other people's amazoid blogs;

(b) starting a blog which I was never happy with as I'm neither an HTML designer nor a sub-editor so, aesthetically, it resembled a badger's arse;

(c) writing posts which took all evening and did nothing except bore ME senseless on the subject;

(d) leaving the post hanging there in cyberspace littered with typos, factual errors and broken pieces of HTML;

(e) checking in occasionally to find there are still no comments aside from the ones sent by spambots selling the drug CiralexQ2000, which promised to get me 'a rock hard clitoriz that would smash down wallz'. Now, I'm not a prude but this sounded kind of painful. I feel sad every time I get an email telling me someone has subscribed to my Posterous.com blog as, statistically, they have more chance of seeing me opening for Lady Gaga at Vatican-Rockz Festival than finding a new post there. I found Twitter instead.

Twitter, however, is an instant way of spreading excitement. Knee-jerk. A primitive grunt. It honours that basic human instinct we share of wanting to turn other humans on to the things we love too. I love watching tweeters making Spotify playlists for friends they've never actually met on the other side of the world, or offering to post them copies of books they've just finished. I watch gruff looking men, brains addled by the sugar rush of a fine knickerbocker glory, wanting the world to note down the name of this LIFE-CHANGING ice-cream parlour in case you're ever passing by:

Gravediggerpete1 The Snickers-amaretto helter skelter sundae is awesome. I think I'm having a heart attack.

Twitter is honed to create genuine word-of-mouth buzz; it's real people telling other real people who tell other people the things that make their hearts soar. And it doesn't have to be fresh, brand-new things. It can be older things or positively ancient things you just weren't in the right headspace to get until now. My Twitter timeline turned me on to Nick Drake, Neu!, the novels of Nancy Mitford, Mike Mitchell's art, the comedy of Katt Williams and Rob Delaney. The plain fact is this: a nicely worded tweet to me, from a tweeter I trust and admire, suggesting I try something because they've thought about it and they think I'd really like it is worth more than any multimillion-dollar advertisement featuring near-nude models, exploding jeeps and CGI wisecracking pigs placed in premium ad time in the middle of my favourite TV show. I've bought things promoted by talking CGI pigs tons of times. Those pigs lie. What DOES make me go and see a movie is when that funny tweeter from Chicago @sideshowbobbit, the guy who I know loves J. D. Salinger and Kate Bush's 'Hounds of Love', who I sat up late with on Twitter watching Oscar 2011 Red Carpet fashion – when HE says he's just been to see a movie and it really cheered him up, well, that's who I listen to. He's not on anyone's pay roll. He's not selling it to me, he's 'putting me on to it'. This is a very different thing.

Stick your BUZZ up your AZZ

Obviously, the second that marketing and PR departments learned of Twitter 'word-of-mouth buzz', it gave birth to a zillion boring 'orchestrated Twitter buzz' campaigns. Now all PR/ad/marketing meetings must involve a section where someone hapless drones on about 'boosting online presence' by 'creating a buzz on Twitter with specifically consumer tailored hashtag viral video blah blah bork', while the others around the table nod in agreement. And I don't blame PRs for telling clients that Twitter will change their lives. Just making the right noises about Twitter keeps lots of clients gurgly and malleable, like turning up in the seal house at London Zoo with a bucket of delicious herring.

If I was a PR I'd promise my clients all sorts of tremendous global Twitter-based 'buzz' because:

(a) It sounds like something zeitgeisty and proactive is being done.

(b) It's free. Especially when I hand the Twitter stream which took me 47 seconds to set up over to your office junior to run.

(c) Hardly anyone on your board of directors understands Twitter, which means I can make all sorts of triumphant promises about how one tweet about your company, Colin's Colon Cleansing Cookies, will lead to Kim Kardashian, Piers Morgan and 50 Cent retweeting your brand name to high heaven, causing a snowballing Twitter-buzz and increasing your brand awareness by 137%!!!

I would prove the 137% growth with a graph I invented,

drew with crayons and coloured in all pretty on the tube journey to your offices.

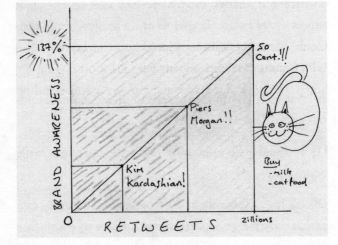

Here's why your rubbish corporate Twitter-orchestrated buzz campaign will probably not work:

(a) Setting up a stiff-looking Twitter page about Colin's Colon Cleansing Cookies and then 'following' hundreds of strangers will, in most cases, lead to them blocking and reporting you as spam instantly. Other tweeters may stare momentarily at your boring page full of 'teaser tweets' which a six-year-old girl recovering from a Bonfire Night eye-injury could figure out is an advert for your product.

(b) Sending tweets to people saying 'HEY, we're Colin's

Colon Cleansing Cookies. Follow us back for some great news!!' is basically just cold-calling people, except in their @mentions column when they're most probably on downtime trying to watch *American Idol* and LOL at Steven Tyler's face. If this is me, I'm already finding Colin's Colon Cleansing Cookies as annoying as the UPVC conservatory company who insist on ringing my house to check if I'd like a quote on a free-standing gazebo when I'm watching *Coronation Street*. And, believe me, this is pretty ruddy livid. In fact, I'm sure the UPVC guys have tapes of some of those phone calls which they play at the Christmas office party. LIVID.

(c) But – HANG ON – what if we send free boxes of Colin's Colon Cleansing Cookies to celebrities with lots of followers so they tweet about them? This is actually not a bad idea.[4]

---

4 I know lots of celebrities and, honestly, they are the biggest bunch of easily corruptible, over-indulged give-me-the-moon-on-a-stick-for-nothing-as-I-can-read-an-autocue grabbing ne'er-do-wells you could ever have the misfortune to meet. Every day is Easter Bunny Sunday to celebrities as they sit permanently on plumped velvet cushions in bay windows clutching binoculars and waiting for dispatch bikes to arrive laden with free things they've been sent purely for being lovely, lovely them, which they then leaf through in incandescent coal-eyed fury because it wasn't bigger and in more colours. PR companies, dig deep! Keep these celebs in the undeserved free shit they so richly deserve!

So you send over your box of Colin's Colon Cleansing Cookies to a Twitter celeb mainplayer with 50K followers and then wait for your reply tweet saying 'WOW THESE ARE THE YUMMIEST THINGS EVER.'

And you wait and you wait and you wait. The problem here is that the celeb is under no obligation to tweet about it, and if they do tweet you've no control over what the silly sod says. Of course, you can shove a celebrity an envelope full of money and pay them to tweet, and lots of them do, but Twitterers weren't born yesterday; we can tell by the style, tone and clipped insincerity captured in 140 characters when a famous person is just pressing send on an advert.[5] And we don't like it.

5 I still laugh about one blonde leading lady of a frothy West End musical who one evening began tweeting the name of a posh health retreat she just HAD to recommend to her 150,000 followers. 'Such an awesome time in this really great spa!' she tweet-bleated in the manner of a woman enjoying a freebie. Hilariously, this gave way as the weekend drew on, with more off-brand messages about being 'bloody starving'. And then finally drunken tweeting at midnight about taking a taxi to the nearby village pub for steak and kidney pudding and chips. Not only had she rinsed the PR for a free £2,000+ trip, she'd spelled out to her 150k normal-folk followers exactly what they feared about booking into such a place: it was a regime of starvation, sobriety and, seeing as she was tapping on her phone every five damn minutes, boredom. I'll pass, thanks.

(d) OK, so we won't bother with celebs. You'll set up . . . a Twitter hashtag about Colin's Colon Cleansing Cookies! And everyone in the world will join in with this shared bit of hilarity. It'll capture the hearts and minds of the Twittersphere and your cookies will sell LITERALLY like hot cakes by the billion and we'll all be millionaires overnight!

Oh, hang on. No, it won't.

This is because hashtags, in my opinion, are great for two things:

(i) Helping people who are sharing the same experience find each other. This could be everyone who is watching *The Apprentice* – #apprentice – or everyone who is attending the British Red Squirrel Conference, #britsquirconf.

(ii) Tweeters just being silly, for sheer LOLZ making up #analjamesbondfilms or #youknowyoufartedbad hashtags.

Twitter is probably not going to want to play your ingenious #ilovecolinscookies game because that's just an advert.

Every hour of the day I watch Twitter buzz campaigns trying, crashing then burning in their attempt to take hold of my timeline. I always think this is a terrible shame as I'm sure, at one point in every campaign, several people involved were fooled into depending on it, believing falsely that everyone *else* knew what they were talking about because they mentioned tweeting Stephen Fry and starting one of them viral buzz wotnots and becoming a global trend wotsit hashcake. The harsh truth is that instead of boosting your product, Twitter can DESTROY. In many ghoulish ways, Twitter is a marketing person's darkest nightmare. If your product sucks and Twitter word begins to spread, well, it's nigh impossible to shut up. Twitter has turned the most powerful PR people into Web 3.0 King Canutes roaring at a sea of electronic ROFLs.[6]

6 So damaging is negative tweet wildfire that some PRs fight hard to ban products being discussed on Twitter before the official launch. Movie studios have started bandying about 'Twitter embargoes' forbidding tweets on their great new movie until the official opening night. This says much about the power of Twitter and even more about movie studios' confidence in green-lighting another multimillion-dollar Jennifer Aniston rom-com where Aniston plays a kookie, terminally single woman with no lines as good as Rachel from *Friends* for 127 seat-chewing minutes.

7. Meet your brain twins

It was the social aspect of Twitter that intoxicated me from the very off.

Here, I could see, was social networking at its most honed and zippy. Goodbye mooching about message-boards with their repetitive locals, in-fighting and power-mad moderators. Begone Facebook, with your awkward formal 'friend acceptance' policy and eons of admin. Welcome to Twitter: the spiritual home of globally ranging mindless chit-chat and larking about. The saviour of procrastinating homeworkers, stuck-at-home parents, folk with mobility issues, the inherently hilarious yet terminally shy, people with important things to say and many others with bugger-all to say but a funny way of doing it. It's a form of 'going out' for the tremendously sociable who, in truth, can't be arsed to leave the house. I fall very much into this category.

I find 'going out' to be an extremely arduous task, involving showering, pondering which message my outfit should emit, fang-brushing, antler scraping, plus a complex dressing process involving various boob-lifting and beehive-steadying aids.

Going out involves frantic circuits of the house mumbling, 'Keys? Keys? OK, found keys . . . Phone? Phone? Oh, it's got no power. OK, keys again. Phone? Purse? Keys.' And all this is usually followed by a period of lying in a fetal position mumbling, 'None of these clothes fit! Someone . . . someone is sneaking into this house . . . and SWAPPING them for a size smaller to demean me! Oh god. I can't be ARSED!'

There's none of this mither when socialising on Twitter. No encounters with public transport. No risk of uninvited penises introduced to the small of my back, nor tiresome chumps with explosives splattering me to the four corners of the Central Line. Ahhhh, Twitter. Just me and the universe sat on the sofa. Stop in, log in and you're good to go.

And Twitter is sublime for making buddies. Yeah, I said 'buddies'. 'Buddy' feels like the right word. Twitter people feel like 'buddies' to me, rather than the more formal-sounding 'friend' or the rather long-winded *People off the internet whom I have realised – via an unconsciously communicated mesh of mutual likes, dislikes and idiosyncrasies in their personality which I either empathise with or am intrigued by – that I really get along with, and whom I continue to chit-chat with in under 140 characters every day, and at all hours of the day and even on Christmas Day, despite many of them living very far away from me, and me not knowing much about their real life at all, aside from what they've told me, which may or may not be entirely true, because let's face it no-one is 100% quite what they seem on Twitter, we all edit our persona and show the things we want to show, which I don't mind as it's only Twitter and I like what this person and I have together, it's all good.* This is a bit of a mouthful, so I prefer 'buddy'.

Alliances made on Twitter can be the stuff of pure joy. How wonderful it would be if Twitter was the web application which finally obliterated people's reticence to discuss their internet buddies in real life. There's still definitely a taboo.

It puzzles me how many people still believe 'friendship' or at least bonhomie conducted in cyberspace isn't a valid form of social contact, but, say, being thrown together at an NCT group, or in halls of residence, or because your desks at work face on to each other, is. Or that anodyne small talk with a neighbour is 'genuine social stimulation', whereas chatting over Twitter with someone 6,000 miles away who loves *Top Gun* and Jefferson Airplane as much as you do is just lonely, dysfunctional nerds clashing in cyberspace. This, to my mind, is idiotic. It's time for us all to come out of the closet about our secret internet chums.

Via the greatness of Twitter I've met several forms

of my cosmic brain, people such as @scouserachel, @soul_of_twit, @betsymartian, @eoschater, @Wadey-Wade, @hoskas and many, many more. Twitter friendships are a thing of joy. They're not built on geographical logistics, workplace convenience, family loyalties or ongoing guilt trips; they're built largely on electronic thin air and a mutual love of dissecting life's minutiae and laughing at stupid stuff. You like laughing at terrible children's choirs? I LOVE laughing at terrible children's choirs! Here, internet buddy, have this YouTube clip of the Oklahoma Under-12 Singing Squad murdering 'Ave Maria'! Let us laugh together while stood in kitchens at either end of Great Britain waiting for dinnertime pasta to boil. Oh, go on. Life is short, let us smile more about nothing much, we'll all be worm food by 2080.

I met my Twitter buddy @scouserachel when we bonded over mutual interest in three crucial world issues:

(a) TV soap character Ronnie Mitchell from *EastEnders* and her crazy-ass hormonal antics.

(b) The ongoing saga of 'Wake Me Up Before You Go-Go' singer turned Wacky Racer George Michael.

(c) The bubblings of the *Daily Mail* online showbiz site.

My curiosity about @scouserachel was first piqued by

her avatar,[7] a blurred photograph taken outside a pub of her accosting Spider Nugent from *Coronation Street*. Or at least Martin Hancock, the man who played Spider in the soap in the 90s. To the other 160 million people in Twitterland, this would mean little, but to me, the fact 'Scouse Rachel' was not only the sort of person who recognised Spider from *Corrie* in a dark street in 2009, but would then chase him and manhandle him into a 'grope and grin' fan shot, indicated we had fundamental things in common (e.g. a love of a good, silly night out and 20/20 recall for soap folk currently residing in the Where Are They Now? file).

@scouserachel and I often hang out with @soul_of_twit. I know @soul_of_twit lives somewhere in Wales, though I have never demanded specific details from her as, to me, Twitter friendships aren't about that. I've no idea what she looks like, although I envision her with blonde bobbed hair. I do, however, know 100% that, the same as me, she likes laughing at old pictures

7 This is a fine example of why Twitter avatar choice is crucial. I always ensure my avatar features me caked in make-up and festooned in diamonds, so suggesting I'm perpetually en route to the launch of my own fragrance/dinner with Liz Hurley at The Ivy. This masks the truth that I'm usually at home clad in baggy-kneed George of Asda leggings writing a column in a deadly silent office which, as I type this footnote, resembles some sort of cat anaesthetic recovery ward.

of Spandau Ballet, and she likes Björk (and has done since the Sugarcubes era). She likes the Dylan Moran sit-com *Black Books*, Nora Ephron columns and watching *MasterChef* and laughing about the manner in which judge Gregg Wallace tastes puddings.[8]

I have small, sometimes surreal yet oddly meaningful connections with hundreds of Twitter buddies. People like @WadeyWade. He agrees with me that the early

---

8 My Twitter memories of meeting @soul_of_twit start in 2008, around six months after Manchester music svengali Tony Wilson died. I tweeted a link to a blog post by another writer I'd been looking at, featuring Wilson's newly unveiled, tastefully designed gravestone with a small write-up about the making of the stone. Rather movingly, the comments section below the photo had been filled with heartfelt tributes to the memory of Wilson. Of his contribution to music, to culture, how he influenced working-class people to broaden their minds and revolt against the premise that art is the pastime of the privileged. Apart from one comment slap bang in the middle of the thread from a disgruntled font nerd which simply said 'TYPEFACE?' I'm not sure where @soul_of_twit came from but I know on that day we were united in cyberspace hysterics over 'TYPEFACE?' and its one-word ability to sum up everything you need to know about a certain type of pedantic, ever-unsatisfied, point-missing internet comment-thread twunt. I've been buddies with @soul_of_twit ever since. We still mumble 'TYPEFACE?' at each other on Twitter to cheer each other up. Twitter heaves and groans 24/7 with intra-tweeter in-jokes such as these. Do other people have a folder on their laptop of jpegs with silly names like martinkempintrunks.jpg and shitmastercheftrifle.jpg simply to pull out in case of Twitter emergency? Or is that just me?

1980s was a top-drawer time in British music (we share YouTube links of Human League on *Top of the Pops* and anecdotes about Soft Cell). @TrishByrne lives somewhere in Ireland; she takes in homeless dogs and trains them for rehoming. The woman is a frickin' saint. I love reading her musings on her newest project and about them leaving for good homes. It cheers me up. Good news does happen in the world.

I don't know much about @liz_buckley except she writes a good pithy tweet. @JennyJohnsonHi5 lives in Texas. She has a lot of deadly funny one-liners about being a step-mother. I know @IAmMamaMya lives somewhere in America. We often cross paths in cyberspace as I'm getting up mega-early to write columns and she's just en route to bed. @Truett is a fashion student in Chicago – I like watching his work in process. Will I ever meet these people? I'm not sure. Perhaps after a decade of making 'buddies' over the internet, Twitter has brought me to a place where friendship no longer depends on building up to an ultimate goal of face-to-face contact.

For every lovely buddy I've made on Twitter, like the ones I mention above, I've lost, unfollowed or forgotten two dozen more. I love that Twitter allows us to monitor in real-time the ongoing brain patterns, personality shifts and belief mutations in human beings. People do change, and Twitter lets us see that day by day in tweeters. If people I follow begin to nauseate me or depress me with tweets full of ego, anger, meanness or blatant ass-kissing, I often quietly duck out. Once we were buddies, seconds later they don't exist in my timeline, and within days they no longer exist for me at all. That's Twitter.[9]

8. Women on Twitter

A cyber-room of one's own

On Twitter I feel something that I feel very rarely in the rest of the world: that my sex is 100% equally repres-ented. For every quickfire 'King of Banter' man there is an equally fast-talking woman. In fact, it's arguable that, in Twitterland, you hear from the sharp, eloquent wo-men MORE than you do from the men – womenfolk simply seem more inclined to start the 'chatting'. When the ladies of Twitter get going their conversations spill on and on over hours, attracting more varied speakers and opinions, spinning off into counterarguments and anec-

9   WARNING: Unfollowing people on Twitter may possibly lead to receiving 'The terrible oh why have you unfollowed me boo-hoo hissyfit email of doom'. (For details of this, see the chapter entitled 'The terrible oh why have you unfollowed me email of doom'.)

dotal evidence, spanning over continents, with the occasional male voice piping up: 'This is brilliant. You lot should be on *Loose Women*.' Which doesn't quite honour the fact that that he's been quietly observing a really bloody funny debate on the idiocy of Premier League footballer superinjunctions argued by a load of fortysomething women with law degrees, newspaper editing experience and women that brought up four kids and are now running companies.

These debates/banter sessions come and go, intermixed with gripes about pricey non-chip nail varnishes, requests for instructions on how to cook monkfish, links to some piece about a stupid fashion trend that all women of sane mind have already decided is unwearable, plus a caustic glance at the new Booker shortlist. Millions of women being sharp, wise, practical amusing. At the age of 35 I felt like someone had opened a gate into a fantastic secret garden full of gobby Amazonians. I knew these women existed, I knew they were out there, I met them day to day, but while leafing through magazine pages or watching TV it's hard to feel particularly satisfied about our progress towards being thought of as 'equals'.

I know I'm thankful every day to Twitter for giving me a platform to say pretty much whatever I want. On television, women are still used as screen parsley stuck on the side of the plate. No-one would really notice if you scraped them into the bin. I recall a famous TV chef's Christmas special on Channel 4 last year where the chef and a flurry of blokey celebs all stood round flaming turkeys and made quips about brandy butter, then at the end Charlotte Church was wheeled on in a mini-dress to sing. Men 'bantering' is a very sellable concept; women bantering is a ratings-killing noise apparently and, besides, we have *Loose Women*. On light-entertainment shows we appear as grinning, semi-mute imbeciles, chosen for being ex-models or wives of footballers, while the menfolk on screen are selected for being 'good TV presenters' and 'safe pairs of hands' in charge of valid thoughts and setting the agenda.

It is quite normal on British TV to see whole hours devoted to men chatting solely to other men about political issues, or men around tables on a Saturday night or Sunday morning bantering about football, or men standing around cars on *Top Gear* mumbling, 'Um, car good! It go fast!' There aren't any shows where you can guarantee to see groups of wry, opinionated women. Why would anyone want to watch that? 'But you've got *Loose Women*!' the men shout, running in from adjoining rooms like a Greek chorus to remind me, some clutching an A2-size picture of a miniature Chihuahua puppy sleeping on its back to distract me from my

Millie Tant whining. So I switch on BBC1, BBC2 or Channel 4 on any evening and there's game shows, some of which have run for decades, where five or more men, all in their 40s or 50s, none with any specific aesthetic splendour – in fact, some will actually look like a large lump of celeriac dressed in a Lyle & Scott sweater – simply 'banter' intelligently with a loose quiz show format. Occasionally one woman might be permitted to join them – sometimes the retired pop star Jamelia – whom everyone will quickly agree wasn't funny and that is why women can't play at all. 'But you've got *Loose Women*!' every man in Britain reading this is shouting at my stupid female head. 'God, she does go on. She sounds like one of them feminists. She probably needs a shag.' So then I shove my annoying wimmins-lib face into the *Radio Times*, brimming with 'Travel-Adventure' shows starring Dom Jolly or Ewan McGregor or Ben Fogle or George Lamb or Rory McGrath or Paddy McGuinness or Robson Green or some other manly man with his manly friends going on an amazing freshwater fishing adventure where they just basically gad about because the show is really all about 'banter'. They natter on about music and their university days, and they meet locals and have a madcap scrape with a combine harvester, which is lovely and inoffensive; in fact, it's soothing to the eyes.

I like silly shows like this, but there are NO shows where three women over 50 go out in a rowing boat just to faff about and banter. There are no game shows where six potato-shaped women sit in a row playing a complex word game. There are no light-entertainment shows where one rowdy maverick woman is the anchor and some weedy pretty boy 15 years her junior, in fake tan, sits by her side saying mostly chuff-all. TV executives will never allow it; they will mutter that people find it off-putting, they will say women don't want to watch other women, they will say finding women who can really talk is very hard and they will probably get out some Venn diagrams and bar charts to prove it, and the incisive findings of a focus group from Rotherham who gave comments like 'Wimmin int funny, is this pizza free like, wat all of it?' But then you log on to Twitter and there are millions and millions of us. Women thinking and sparring and also, interestingly, making men laugh. Yes, real live females with boobs and fallopian tubes issuing acerbic swipes on Cameron's foreign policy, spitting out wry sideways looks at EU initiatives, debating the merits of giving a second date to a man off *Guardian* Soulmates with a Mario Kart neck tattoo, and single-handedly beating a load of men at a hashtag game based around the theme #constipatedTSEliot.

Twitter is full of sharp, opinionated women. Or, as men

tend to call us, 'sassy'.[10] To my mind, Twitter gave me and large swathes of women a space to talk, interact and represent ourselves on a level we're not generally afforded.

Sample work request: 'Hey, Grace, we're looking for you to write some material for our show on why wigs on men can be really naff, but we need it to be something extra-sassy. Y'know, a real shoot-from-the-lip affair!'

'Dear Dicksplash from Vibe Productions, I am delighted you want to employ me and my 15 years' experience as a comedy writer. Incidentally, do you pitch to Charlie Brooker in a tone as if you want him to totter in dressed as Doris Day in a fringed bra with guns in holsters while everyone cups their face in wonderment at the incredible back-chatting man? Actually, I don't think I can do this. I'm all sassied out this week. I'm going to stay at home and bake cupcakes. I need to concentrate on my ganache icing.'

What an amazing thing: turns out we can write as funnily and sharply as men. Before Twitter, which now sates my need for womanly chat every day, I would walk into

---

10 I hate being called 'sassy'. The only reason 'sassy' still exists to denote a 'woman who can verbally spar and issue droll one-liners at the same level as a man' is because we're so unused to seeing her we haven't invented any other words since the 1950s.

newsagents in search of something 'for a woman to read', stare at the screaming wall of 'women's interest magazines' and wonder whether I was really a female at all. In all seriousness, during my teens and 20s it often worried me that I was wired differently to other women. Things that to this day still worry me that I might be a man whenever I visit WH Smith and gaze up at the magazines are:

(a) I do not give a shit about Jennifer Aniston.

I loved her in *Friends*, but I could not be less arsed about whether Jennifer Aniston is sad, happy, alone, dating, un-lucky in love again, bearing up after heartbreak, has a stomach upset, is on holiday, has been seen wearing a nice dress, or is helping Courteney Cox cope with her heartbreak. I DON'T CARE. If you cold-called me and asked me to help you with your survey entitled *Shit I Think About Jennifer Aniston*, I would go for the box 'I couldn't give a fuck' every single time.

(b) See also: Sienna Miller. You know that girl who went out with Jude Law and then didn't and then did again? I don't care about her. I don't even know what her job is now. Professional cock-holder for Jude Law? I don't know, I can't even be bothered to Google her name, such is my level of non-commitment to Sienna Miller. What I do know, however, is that in WH Smith at any given time there will be at least five Sienna Miller covers staring down at me, and the headlines will say something like: 'Sienna's shocking call to Sadie!'

And if I do approach the counter and part with £2.50 (maybe I'm displaying the first signs of some aneurism) it will transpire that Sienna Miller called Sadie Frost one night last month, a source close to the pair confessed, to tell her that her burglar alarm was ringing, to which Sadie said, 'Oh,' and turned it off. This piece of household admin will be stretched out for 2,000 words.

I cannot comprehend a world where men would read a front-page headline that says 'ROONEY QUITS FOOTBALL!' and pay £2.50 to read it, and be perfectly satisfied that it turned out that Rooney 'quit' playing football in a manner of speaking at 5pm one night because Colleen said his fish fingers were ready for tea, and then returned to football at 9am the next morning. So he didn't quit. In man-land, an editor would get away with playing this trick a maximum of one time before someone called the office and threatened to feed him to pigs. And quite rightly so. One of the great things about Twitter is if you 'break' a story which turns out to be a load of old crap, people will tell you so.

(c) Those 'Steal Sienna's/Jennifer's/Sadie's Look!' fashion pages. I don't want to.

Here is a picture of Sadie in a hat. This is a very, very popular hat now and here is the place where you can buy it. It is £800 pounds. Don't baulk at the price as it is a 'signature piece' – and here is a picture of Alexa Chung wearing the hat on a boat with a man's jumper and some denim shorts and another subheading reminding us she is 'the coolest woman in the world'. A-ha, you want the hat now, don't you? Well, you can't have it, they only made six, so you need to call up Milan and put your name on a waiting list!

(d) I don't care about Fashion Week.

When I hear the words 'fashion week', I feel like a failure in the woman stakes. I cannot emit the requisite amount of glee at the thought of finding out 'next season's colours', or the chance to gaze upon pages and pages of gargoyle-faced fashion supremos and their bony retinues stood in the 'party pages' looking grumpy and hungry. I do like 'wearing clothes'; in fact, I do it most days and am, indeed, as I type this, 'dressed'. Perhaps it's because I worked with a lot of these types of people and many of them wouldn't squeeze out a spare piss on to the chubby, 12k-a-year-earning general public if a pile of them were ablaze outside their Rue De Frou Frou fashion house.

I have an especially low interest in the 20 or so accompanying pages of 'spring/summer' vestments that you would look a bit 'mutton' in past the age of 19, but would only be able to afford when you have the earning potential of a child-free, 44-year-old CEO power-lesbian. I am not interested in 'think pieces' about whether size 12–14 women should be allowed to go down the catwalk and be able to easily find clothes in shops. I don't need to 'think' about that. Only a gibbering dunderhead has to think about that. I am not fussed about looking at pictures of very thin teenagers wrapped in £9,000 dresses who've been dieting for weeks pre-Fashion Week, living on fresh air, laxatives and lines of cocaine given to them by photographers' assistants who take advantage of them. But, hey ho, woah Gracie, keep it light, it's all good fun, and LOOK, IT'S ALEXA CHUNG IN THAT FAMOUS HAT AGAIN! ISN'T SHE PRETTY? She's the coolest woman in the world. (Oh, screw this. If you want me I will be on Twitter. *Love, @gracedent*.)

Also file under 'Don't Care':

– A harrowing story of an ectopic pregnancy.

– A telling tale about a woman whose body clock ran out before she had the time to have babies.

– Woman lost weight (by consuming less calories and moving around more).

– Woman puts on weight (by going on holiday and having more food than normal).

– A list of signs I need to look out for to check if my husband is cheating on me.

– A double-page shopping spread on scented candles.

– A rock star's wife telling me how she did up her ten-bedroom farmhouse by sourcing locally made antique lace and sticking organic goose poo on all the beams and whoopie-do she's got a book out about it for £35 called *My Silk Heaven: Sally Simper's Country Cottage*, and I should buy it.

Twitter makes me feel like more of a success at femininity as it's full of women who laugh at this type of rot too. It's also been a godsend for letting me write unfettered, unformulated thoughts about my experience as a female that I would have literally nowhere else to shove.

To this day, there are still only a few lovely editors who let me write as I want. Over the past fifteen years, when writing for a female audience I have found my writing subtly – and to my mind completely unmaliciously – edited to make me sound 'more like a woman'. For example, cultural references that might be thought a bit challenging for women are snipped out. Take the other day, when I wrote a line that ended 'a large gin and tonic and back-to-back *Boardwalk Empire*'. In print it appeared as 'a nice glass of wine and a facemask'. I wrote a joke for a women's mag about dancing at Christmas in my kitchen to Jona Lewie and found it in print changed to 'Mariah Carey'. (In my experience, women are not trusted to have any knowledge of music, so therefore wouldn't understand the reference to Lewie's lyric 'I wish I was at home for Christmas'. If I had typed that I'd been dancing to James Blunt it would most probably have been left, as even though James Blunt has never had a famous Christmas single, women would not be thought to know this fact, but would see the words 'James Blunt' and feel soothed.) I penned a one-liner about my attitude to friendships being 'loyal like a dog (without the urge to wash oneself intimately in public)', to find the end of the joke cropped for a female audience to read simply as 'my friendship is loyal like a dog'.

When I write for women I often find extra lines put in to soften my tone. To save me from myself, perhaps. 'Maybe I'm being harsh here, ladies . . .' I hear myself apparently saying, or 'Playing devil's advocate for a second here, girls . . .' to soften my thrust. OK, I might be rattling out 1,500 words on the insanity of spending £6,000 on a handbag when 25% of the kids in your district live in poverty, but, hey, this is a think piece for women so please keep it 'chatty and warm', so as not to alienate readers who want to see you as a 'sassy best friend'. I wonder if men get told to soften the tone of think pieces for fear that the poor male reader might feel under attack? Or are they allowed to be as pointy-tongued as they want, as men trust other men to lap up a few truthbombs and realise they're talking about some other jerk anyway?

Unformulated women's thoughts

Twitter gives me the chance to instantly say things that are happening to me that I'd not be able to place elsewhere. I'm not promising profundities. Just knee-jerk daftness, but with no editorial interference. I found that as I typed things like this, women poured out of the woodwork. Here are some tweets that got mega-RTs, and a little about what I was thinking:

> **gracedent** Men i don't know: i don't care if it's a balmy night and it's last orders. it's NEVER ok to high five me on the size of my baps.

I am constantly amazed at what men think it's all right to shout at me in the street if I'm alone. I try to tell them there is a subtle but definite difference between a cheeky, impromptu 'hello, darling, you look lovely' (which is nice), and someone simply winding down the window of their Vauxhall Rascal in a traffic jam and shouting 'MELONS' three feet from my face (which if guns were more available in Britain I would be doing 15 years for by now). I used to tweet about it more, but it always gets a lot of angry replies from men moaning about 'political correctness gone wrong', and I have learned from experience on Twitter that I'm not going to change any man's view on 'female strength' via 140 characters, and going round to their house to beat them with a chair is not always possible.

> **gracedent** It must be cold in the 3am regent street ipad queue. especially when you've been pressure-washed and run over by a streetcleaner.

I tweeted this passing the iPad queue on the way back from working on a late-night talk-radio show. Although I may sound like I'm deriding these Mac nerds sleeping on the kerb, the truth is I'm a solid brushed-aluminium Mac junkie myself and had to give myself a good talking to so as to NOT jump out the cab and spend the night huddled in a group with them, being urinated on by tramps, just for a lucky opportunity to give Apple another £700 for something which doesn't quite work as well as it should, and which I'll feel duped into upgrading in 18 months. I wish this was a joke. It's not.

> **gracedent** Push it by salt n pepa will never stop sounding good.

This is a very typical @gracedent-slightly-drunk-in-a-2am-mini-cab-whizzing-home-through-London tweet. I'm pretty sure when Cheryl James and Sandra Denton were laying down 'Push It' with Cameron Paul back in the 80s, pouring on lycra trousers and long red boots, sculpting their hair, the audience they had in mind for the song was a small spam-skinned English woman with her shoes off in a taxi doing 'lost in the moment funk overbite' while tweeting to her friends who work for the *Guardian*. I'm pretty sure that's how it went.

> **gracedent** Oh, piss off 'Earth Hour'. have a shower in the dark, save a puffin whatever.

As a Twitter village elder I have a very low tolerance for people coming around these parts talking about 'fancy ideas wot have tried and failed before'. And I have sat through the run-up to Earth Hour on many occasions only to come to the hour in question and see east London lit up like the Las Vegas strip on the night the Chemical Brothers swung by with an extra-special light-and-laser show. JOG ON.

> **gracedent** i watched The Truth About Lions tonight on BBC1. it turns out they're just tigers in joke shop Tina Turner wigs. soz for spoiler.

This is totally true.[11] We also found out that wasps are just 'naughty bees' and that owls always look that furious because someone sneaked into an Owl General Meeting and spoiled *Battlestar Galactica* for them.

> **gracedent** One second you're the in crowd and everything is glam hotels and parties and being fabulous and then very quickly you're ancient and gone.

I tweeted this after the death of a Hollywood siren and I was watching one of her old friends, now in his 80s, recounting what a blast they all had in the 1960s when they were bright, young, gorgeous, intercontinental, jetsetting

---

11 Not true. Lions are not tigers. Do not write this in any GCSE exam.

film stars, all shagging each other secretly and having expensive divorces and buying homes in the Hollywood Hills and collecting Oscars and drinking champagne and knocking back Valium and having dinner with Elvis and Frank Sinatra and owning lions as pets. And now he could barely stand up and the woman he was talking about was dead. Life passes in a blink. Even if you're the hippest people on earth.

> **gracedent** RED TROUSERS? (a) are you santa? (b) did they come from a post-disaster humanitarian drop? (c) do you work in a fun 50s diner? (d) NO.

I very often see a fashion trend emerging and feel a lot like Chandler in that episode of *Friends* where he's made a bet with Rachel, Monica and Joey that he won't make fun of his friends any more, and then Ross shows up in leather trousers.[12]

> **gracedent** Are there enough women in britain with roaring PMT to keep Desigual open?

12 To my mind there is a scene in *Friends* which can explain every human emotion known to mankind. I invite you to test me on this on Twitter.

Sometimes I pop into the fashion store Desigual, just out of sheer curiosity to see what traffic-stoppingly hilarious garments are cluttering their shelves this month. Desigual appear, to my uncultured, non-fashionista mind, to corner the market in the 'demented 18th-century Spanish travelling circus ringleader' look. If there's ever an occasion in your diary where a long, dark, purple maxi skirt in ruched velour with a stonewash clown's face leaping out of a pleat, a non-removable conch-belt and a multi-petticoat trim would be perfect, then Deisgual is for you. You can match it with one of their tie-dye peasant tops in gold, amber and azure with leather tassels and faux-ivory beaded fringing. I tweeted this while sitting in Pret A Manger on Regent Street one Sunday morning, watching a queue of women waiting to be allowed in to shop. I can only imagine they were all from the same women's prison or boarding school and their menstrual cycles had aligned. Shortly after this tweet, I had a message from someone involved with Desigual asking me to get in touch. I thought about whether I wanted to call someone specifically to be screamed at and decided instead to have a Snapple and turn my phone off.

gracedent i'm so glad the super moon has arrived and all the legions of evil lavae I've laid can fully metamorphosise and wage war making me QUEEN.

A 'supermoon' is the coincidence of a full moon (or a new moon) with the closest approach the Moon makes to the Earth on its elliptical orbit, or perigee. Apparently. When such a thing occurred recently Twitter ran en masse towards their bedroom windows squealing, 'Oh my God, isn't the supermooooon amazing!' Well, everyone except me. Since watching the BBC series of *The Day of the Triffids* as a child in the 70s, I refuse to get whipped up in any such inter-planetary-related mass hysteria in case I wake up in the morning to find the whole world blinded and, worse still, being chased to their deaths by a lot of very disgruntled shuffle-footed yucca plants. I tried to warn people on Twitter about the insanity of messing about with the supermoon via my quirky gadabout but everyone ignored me. But they'll learn. They'll all learn.

gracedent When they advertise Treme with 'It's The Wire . . . with trombones' i think, yeah that's what The Wire season 2 needed AN EXPERIMENTAL JAZZ SECTION.

I enjoy verbally attacking Baltimore police drama *The Wire*, not because I dislike it – in fact, I believe it to be some of the finest TV ever made – but just because *Wire* fans are so famous for their thick skin and keen sense of humour that it's just very satisfying to deride it and for us all to enjoy this shared bit of fun. *Wire* fans are a real hoot. They love nothing more than a small, verbose woman made of breasts, hairspray, hormones and ovaries to pour scorn on their favourite show and bandy about that the second series was just a lot of people looking in sea crates and mumbling incoherently, and they ESPECIALLY love it when I make up fake spoilers when they are still halfway through watching Season 3, e.g. 'I think it jumped the shark when Stringer and Omar start the pilates school.' They love this. I always get a very positive response.

> **gracedent** The trick is to never let your mind pursue what Quorn actually is. someone told me it's harvested from Chico's nostrils.

A lot of my friends on Twitter namecheck products in a shameless way to get free shit sent to them. The lengths I've seen people earning a quarter of a million quid a year go to simply to get a £13 dress free is staggering. Others will suddenly begin tweeting furiously about how they love a certain vegetable, cut of meat or dairy product as they've just had £20k+ shoved in their account by the appropriate marketing board to be 'the face of cottage cheese'. I'm not sure what I'm doing wrong – perhaps I give out the air that I can't be trusted to stay on brand message – but no-one ever sends me anything. This, despite my full-throated commitment to electing myself the UK face of Quorn, that weird fake-meat fungus stuff which they apparently grow in silos, and which I eat loads of as it doesn't involve killing any pigs. I happen to like pigs and believe them to be much more intelligent than almost all of the members of the boyband Blue so it pains me to see them die. Still, Quorn steadfastly refused to keep me in the textured fungi-based mycoprotein fake scotch eggs that my level of Twitter regality so richly deserves. Nothing. Not even a pack of Quorn turkey-substitute slices. And I talked about Quorn almost every day for a month, which to my mind means they should have erected me a Quorn 'gingerbread house' with a little fake-chicken path and sizzling not-real-beef roof. Screw you, Quorn, you had your chance.

gracedent Sometimes I go to my brothers' houses, put on The Black Eyed Peas, whip their kids up to a swivel-eyed squealing state, then piss off home.

. . . And that's why everyone loves fun Aunty Grace.

gracedent There is literally nothing imperfect about nicole scherzinger. nothing. She's perfect. I hope she gets recurrent cystitis.

I really mean this. I hate this beautiful cow. If cystitis wasn't an option, I would settle for 'rampant thrush', 'vaginismus' or just a short, non-terminal bout of 'tampon-induced toxic shock syndrome'. I'm not fussy.

gracedent never ruche big boobs! it's like first page rule in the big boob handbook. #oscarnightfashion

I should write the big-boob handbook. I think a lot of stacked women would appreciate it, and we could fool a lot of men into buying it thinking it would be pictures of us oiling our chests while bouncing on a trampoline, when in fact it would be an extended 40,000-word moan on back pain, good shock-absorber bras and the perils of not being able to enter expensive china shops as your tits go on ahead and cause breakages. It would be the least satisfactory 'gentleman's special relaxing time' prop ever.

The truth about childcare

Despite being fed foie-gras-style the belief for 30-odd years that – regardless of my career – having a baby would be the most rewarding thing I could ever do with my life, Twitter appears to tell a slightly different tale. I am not suggesting for a second that Twitter is full of women who don't love their kids with every fibre of their being – it is – but there is an immediacy, a frankness, an off-guardedness, a candour about babies on Twitter which allows for an interesting meta-story to emerge.

Oh God 6 weeks of school holidays save me.

Just spent ten minutes in toilet with ipad pretending to have bad stomach so I can have time off from son.

Jesus Christ are there really 74 different acts at junior school talent night?

GNGNGN. Who decides on these stupid 'Dress up as a children's book character' days?

Twitter tells a daily tale of women entering a state of depression about the prospect of their own children's half-terms. Women travelling to deserted offices over the

Christmas holidays to do fake work projects. Women driven to the end of their tether by the discovery of a two-metre-high *Scooby Doo* pirate ship crayoned on to their living-room wall. Nocturnal Twitter is abundant with sleep-deprived women pacing homes clutching small lumps which are simultaneously pooing, crying and running an inexplicable temperature (which might just be down to the central heating, but on the other hand could be meningitis). To assist teenage girls with their contraception choices, they should be forced to join Twitter and follow @susienewmomma going through her first year with a new baby, with nipples that look like they've been chewed by a basset hound, buying cardigans out of a *Daily Express* insert catalogue as she can't go to shops any more, unable to leave her own baby with the bloke who got her pregnant as he won't stick with the bonkers regime which the unhinged harridans she met on her NCT course are bullying her into. And even if @susienewmomma does leave the house, she has to take a herculean rucksack of organic mashed courgette and baby wipes out with her to maintain this baby, which is presently going through a stage of making a noise like a fire alarm if she doesn't make direct eye contact with it at all times. @susienewmomma has had two hours' sleep in the past fortnight and if she doesn't frighten girls into doing A-levels then nothing will.

The downsides of Twitter

Of course, Twitter addicts love to claim their favourite site is one big constant stream of important, vital ideas. We do this to make our addiction to arsing about on the internet seem less idiotic. Why otherwise would we be checking our phones while crossing three lanes of moving traffic? Why else would we have been asked not to return to yoga for trying to tweet 'I am at yoga doing a downwards dog' while in the downwards dog pose? Because Twitter is CRUCIAL INFORMATION, that's why. Well, OK, more truthfully it is some of the time. And the rest of the time it's full of acres of mind-dissolving, life-robbing bilge. After around 12 months on Twitter, I began to worry about the thousands of pieces of futile crap-o-mation I was exposing my brain to. The twaddlings of egomaniacs, A-grade inanity, adverts, charity begging, tedious social-climbing. The heavy Twitter user, to stay sane, must become an expert hyper-skimreader. And even so, they will still float about their daily life with the remnants of a million terrible tweets still clogging up their brains. Here are some types of tweets that make Twitter, frankly, shitter.

1. Boastposts

Edgyhair32 zomg! I'm named in the top 75 most influential young designers! Mistake??? http://bit.ly/ex1nJl

Meggamommy I cant believe my child can order in Manderine in restaurant. Brains NOT from me!

Septicsam I met Salman Rushdie last night and he said he's a massive fan of my writing. My life = made!!!

Bighead27 RT @lolabanana OMG bighead27 you are such a positive person you totally add to my life. >> me: no way!!!

@gracedent's advice kiosk

Message to boastposters (PLEASE RT)

Are you feeling ever so humble but know you have a duty to mention something to your Twitter friends? Have you been nominated for an award? Are you ever so amazed you've been mentioned in a newspaper or corporate newsletter? Were you out last night and a celebrity bumped into you and remembered your name? Was this a shock? Have you been asked on to a judging panel, and you totally can't believe they asked little old you? Are you taking a dress back to the boutique as it's too big since you started running 10k a day? Have you had so many Follow Fridays that you can't possibly thank everyone individually because you're 'swamped'? Are you group-replying to birthday congratulations in the timeline as your DM box is full? Are you still drunk at work as you got SO drunk last night at the amazing mid-week party you were at? Did someone come and see your lecture or your show or your art exhibition and send you a tweet saying they liked it? Well for heaven's sake RT this praise without delay! We all need to share in the experience of one person quite liking something you're responsible for. It's not like any of us little things have anything else at all going on in our little lives. In fact, better still, why don't you @ in your employer or someone else you want to work for! And you're not just boasting, oh no, perish the thought. You're just communicating that you can't believe anyone thinks this about you, as you're so very, very humble. You're just a geek who got lucky, really. You don't think you're really worth any of this. That's why you're on Twitter 24/7 being a humility-free zone, you massive self-congratulatory knob. SHUT THE FUCK UP. It's not all about you.

Love, @gracedent

Ploughing though other people's boastposts is a serious time-consumer on Twitter. I only wish I didn't find some of the biggest culprits so difficult to unfollow due to their toxic level of ego being bloody fascinating. I'm intrigued by the boastposters' confidence that everyone wants to hear why they personally think they're amazing and have completely lucked out on this life business. Hustle-heavy and empathy-light, the boastposter never bores of their own story and thinks that neither will you. Of course, many celebs, especially male comedians and actors, take boastposting to a higher level of 'lovely me-ness', dispensing with even a cursory nod towards a back story on their announcement or a faux-humble pay-off.

Take @minervemundane here:

Minervemundane Talking about the new show on R4 Today programme. Other people in green room: Tony Blair, Lou Reed.

Minervemundane Pre-recording slot on 'My Big Brain' on itv4 for Thursday's show. Tune in.

Minervemundane My appearance on tonight's 'Good Golly We're So Clever' on BBC4 goes out to-night. Very funny. Tune in.

Minervemundane Me talking about my new show

here in Evening Standard. tinyurl.com/3gtrmfa Very
good review. Very pleased.

Minervemundane On BBC radio scotland tomorrow at 6am. Will be up on iplayer.

@gracedent's advice kiosk

Dear Minerve Mundane

Thank you for keeping us abreast of every appointment
and booking on your agent's 'What is Minerve Mundane
up to today?' spreadsheet. You really are a busy man. One
thing I find puzzling is: Who exactly do you think is the
target audience for this level of detail about your career?
Who indeed is this ardent Minerve Mundane 'random shit
he is doing now' completist you're tweeting to? Are you
tipping off your official archiver? Perhaps I'm wrong and
there really is a Minerve Mundane superfan gobbling up
each tweet you send with the appropriate thigh-rubbing
boggle-eyed ardour, but, mate, do you really want to give
this person your precise whereabouts?

OK, Minerve, I accept that back in the 80s as a teenager
if I loved a comedian or a performer I would indeed make
it my aim to collect and harbour any footage I could of

what they did. I'd fill dusty VHS tapes and scrapbooks and sit in my bedroom nursing burns from hair-crimping appliances mooning over my quarry. But, Minerve: (a) that was the 80s, pre-internet; (b) there was fuck all else to do in Carlisle aside from read *Smash Hits* and eat Slush Puppy; and (c) I held this level of fascination for people like Morrissey or David Bowie, not 'someone who once did a mildly amusing set at the Edinburgh Comedy Festival three years ago and now appears in the UK campaign for cheese triangles'. Bitch – you ain't that interesting.

Love you, @gracedent

2. Smugtweets

Are you experiencing a moment in your life of such Zen-like inner glee and spiritual awareness that you have to share it? You need to smugtweet. Smugtweets are a different animal to boastposts because the tweeter isn't simply bragging but also attempting to teach the world a little lesson.

> **Mellymooch** Log fire blazing, Tuscan stew on the stove, both the boys in my life asleep. BLISS.

@Mellymooch's news would be mildly tweetworthy if she'd just finished hot, rigorous, three-way action with Brazilian twin male models, but we all know that's not the case and her 'two boys' are her husband and her baby (could be her cat), who are snoring in front of *Songs of Praise*. Yes, @Mellymooch may be head of international human resources at Grabbit, Fuckyou and Scrote Global Banking Solutions, but here she is, just a simple girl at home, barefoot, stirring a delicious and nutritious stew, suddenly at one with the insanity of materialism in the face of hard-wired domesticity. Yes, 20 minutes later she'll be using the same phone to relocate a Crewe call centre to India and fire 500 people before Christmas, but during the typing of this tweet she was the Dalai fucking Lama.

> **richiemaldin** My whole family – 4 generations – sitting around the table eating my famous roasties! What life's about!

Yes, @richiemaldin, you win at 'families'. You've got a kitchen big enough to fit a 20-person dinner table and you're on speaking terms with everyone in your family. Yes, you beat all of us barbarians who can't have more than four adults from our bloodline in the same room for

more than half an hour without one sister taking enormous umbrage with another over an imagined grievance,
and your cousin's family outstaying their welcome by 14
to 16 hours. You win.

> **josiedrivel** At the Superkid of the Year Awards – so
> many celebs, but the CHILDREN are the real stars
> here.

Translation: I am at a party getting pissed with celebs
which I was invited to and you weren't but I want you all
to know I'm doing something really good by hanging out
with kids who have cancer.

> **candybutton** Wow. Surveying the grand canyon at
> night really makes me feel humble about my place on
> the planet.

Awww, that's great. You must feel so 'blessy'. Mind you
don't fall in.

3. OMG look at the weather tweets

simoncyst I wish I'd worn my hat today my ears are quite cold.

lucylastic wow the sky is grey in Hackney. Looks like rain.

Twitter bloody loves weather. Twitter loves weather like your gran and her Tuesday Club love weather. Was it a wee bit chilly when you popped to the Post Office? Do you regret wearing thick tights today as it's more clement than you thought? Is it so windy that the trees were moving? Did you think at first that was a raindrop but it turned out to be a hailstone? That's a tweet right here!

celinebong The sun is shining! Woo hoo. It's SUNNY.

lucylastic THE SUN! THE SUN IS IN THE SKY!!

koolkeith Omg The sun makes my street look soooooo beautiful.

All right, I know I'm being slightly mean here. British

tweeters can be forgiven for tweeting wildly about sun-shine as we live in almost continuous grey drizzle, so basically any exposure to vitamin D or stepping free of a fully toggled duffle coat is a BIG DEAL. We get so over-hyped about the sun in the UK that on almost any sunny day it looks like a tribe of Inca sun disciples fuelled on double espressos has taken hold of my Twitter timeline. We worship you, um, flaming fireball! We tweet you in praise!

Of course, on Twitter, the only thing bigger than sun is snow. It only actually takes a light dusting of snowflakes over a small area of south-east England and by 11am Twitter will be laden with flake-size updates, estimated depths and twitpics of usually quite sage business CEOs attaching coal eyes and scarves to anthropomorphised piles of slush, then sliding down hills on tea trays.

Obviously this snow is only important on Twitter if it happens close to London. Or, at a push, perhaps Manchester. Occasionally a tweeter living in a farmhouse near Aberdeen will tweet that it's actually been snowing very heavily for weeks in rural places where no media people live and his whole family has been snowed in and is existing off RAF food drops, but everyone will ignore him in favour of RTing a funny jpeg of two snowmen in Watford who have been positioned to go at it doggy-style. By day two of snow reaching London, Twitter will have decided the snow to be 'a really grave problem' as their feet are getting slightly wet on the way to work and the office refreshment vending machine has run out of hot chocolate.

4. Dudes in a moral panic

panicdood They're trying to take a gay statue away in Cleethorpes!!

panicdood This local newspaper article is trying to mallign women who won't breastfeed! Burn the writer!

panicdood Don't let our Great British Pie disappear!!

panicdood This kindergarten teacher in Delaware saying Creationism is fine to teach kids.

panicdood We need to march on Westminster about Ugangan genital mutilation.

panicdood We need to arrest Robert Mugabi over crimes in Zimbabwe!

panicdood We need to arrest the pope when he comes to Britain for being a massive paedo!

panicdood This high court judge is sort of saying in a roundabout fashion that women shouldn't wear miniskirts.

panicdood Omg the logo on these chocolate biscuits look a bit anti-semetic.

panicdood Let's all call this number and complain and go on a march about these Nazi Hitler biscuits.

panicdood Has no-one remembered WORLD AIDS today PEOPLE ARE DYING?

@gracedent's advice kiosk

OK, dude in a moral panic, I've not even had my first coffee, will you stop bloody shouting at me? I get it. The world is unfair. I've seen *The Color Purple*, I know what goes on. I'm an emotional woman. Believe me, dude, in the brief breaks I had from writing this book for 17 pence an hour (while various publishing-industry people hit me with a stick with a nail in it) I listened to yards and yards of Tori Amos's fairytale-esque screeching, looked at pictures of Congolese child soldiers, sobbed into a Unicef collection envelope and ate only Quorn-pâté baguettes as I disagree with factory farming. Dude, there is no emoticon available to express my sadness at Planet Earth.

But sometimes, dude, dude in a moral panic, I just want to come on Twitter and chat with my friends about the *Daily Mail*'s online showbiz site. Sometimes I just want to laugh at Kim Kardashian's sweaty camel toe in yoga trousers. Sometimes I want to work out who is the most smug, Heidi Klum or Seal, and that time is right now, so stop fucking outrage-bombing my timeline asking me to be livid at stuff. I didn't ask you to march anywhere with me when they cancelled *Friends* re-runs on E4.

pissoffthankyoubyebye, @gracedent

5. Exercise tweet-zzzz

Lycraliz ten-mile run at dawn!! What a beautiful day!!

Ex-raverroy WOW Richmond Park is stunning. Ended up doing 12 miles instead of 8 just to smell the cut grass!

Dj-nutnut Streetslambootyshake class at Soho Gym is SO SO SO amaaaazoid!!!

The many amazing things about exercise are undeniable. All the 'stops you dying young/makes your body look less gross so you get laid more' stuff, that's all good. One of the dangers of exercise is it also releases harmful mood-enhancing chemicals into your brain. I say 'harmful' as they may turn you into an insufferable tosspot, making you almost as high as those people pouring out of that rave you jogged past at 7am who had been eating MDMA powder for six hours. In this state of bliss you think sending tweets about exercise accomplishment is a really good idea.

You forget that most followers reading your tweet give £50 every month to a gym that they couldn't find without a map, and that these people hate you for reminding them about it at 11am when they've just woken up.

Oh, exercise-buzz tweeter, you really think strangers want to read precisely how many kilometres you've just totted up and around which park and whether you found it harder or easier than last time or whether your glutes or your hamstrings are giving you gyp and how many calories you burned down to the closest kilojoule, but believe me they don't. Only your personal trainer is interested in this info and that's cos you pay him to pull the appropriate faces. All you do is make us anxious and sad. In fact, I cried the other day when you tweeted, 'Woo hoo just got my form through for the London Marathon!!' at the thought of the exhaustive details of your training mission and constant prompts for me to dig deep for your really great charity cause – in fact, actually, what am I saying, pass me my purse, I'll sponsor you to STFU.

6. Bong! Guess who's dead?

RIP Liz taylor.

Omg – the queen of hollywood is gone. There will never be another!

Liz Taylor RIP. A part of me died today.

FAIRWELL LIZ! This woman made me who I am. Typing this through a veil of tears.

Clearly celebrities or people of note passing away is always interesting. That's news. We all like fresh news. However, once we've established the fact that someone's breathing no more, the following 48 hours of personal tributes, cloying memories, OTT bewailings and mawkish guff for most of us gets a bit much.

Take Hollywood royal Liz Taylor, for example. Did one woman really deserve so many hysterics chucking themselves headfirst into a Twitter pity party? I accept it came as a real shock to many, what with her always being in such rude and boisterous health. But what amazes me is a lot of these snottering, pyre-jumping sots were actually British. Now, by George, to my mind grieving in this full-throated manner is NOT what our culture is about. Button up, British tweeters! I don't care if Twitter has got us mixing every day willy-nilly with your foreign sorts and your intercontinentals, when it comes to death, we should meet this topic in the traditional way: stiffly and with emotional detachment, a refusal to deal with it, emote or speak about it.

Eventually, after nine days of silence, the mourners typically meet up in a stark crematorium to hear bland tributes led by a vicar who didn't know the dead person, followed by an awkward rendezvous in a creaky hotel function room featuring potted-meat sandwiches, fruit scones and small-talk with octogenarians about who just bought a camper van, during which no meaningful reference needs to be made to the dead person at all.

Emotion-wise, I will allow for a punch-up outside a pub at about 11pm.

Simonsausage RIP Liz. My thoughts are with her friends and family at this difficult time.

Oh, look, Simon has hit his automated 'my thoughts with her friends and family' grief-response button. News just in from Jacko and Bubbles in Twitter heaven. They're reading Twitter and they say 'THANKS DUDE'.

ShowbizSam So sad about Liz taylor I had the privilige of meeting her in 2008.

Betty_boom Gutted about Liz. I was fortunate enough to interview her once for Vogue http://goo.gl/qwVep

@gracedent's advice kiosk

Dear Showbiz Sam

Could you at least wait until the old broad is cold before you begin touting yourself round the TV channels as official media mourner at £100 a soundbite + taxis. Oh, and full marks, Betty, nothing says 'grief' like rushing to re-remind everyone what great showbiz scoops you do.

Love, @gracedent

7. Oh, it's a parody tweet!

Every major news event or pop-culture phenomenon gives birth to a Twitter parody account. Here, a tweeter churns out jokes and one-liners in the supposed style of whichever micro-celeb, terrorist, failing sports star or displaced dictator is riding the zeitgeist that month. Parody tweeters are the web 2.0 version of the bad professional lookalike your boss thinks will brighten up his team motivational away day. Well, if the professional lookalike showed up for said day and stood in the middle of the room shouting continually what a massive stupid dickhead the person they are playing is.

Say, for example, someone impersonates Donald Trump and calls him @shitdonaldtrump. Typically, @shitdonaldtrump will then follow a ton of celebs, spewing out lines in the style of Trump, waiting for one celeb to bite and RT to a mass audience. If the parody site is very of-the-moment, it will gain momentum rapidly, amassing 10,000+ followers in a blink. The parody tweet writer, now experiencing the sugar rush of being a Twitter celeb and having Stephen Fry RT them, quickly becomes consumed with their role and remains on Twitter day and night, tweeting and tweeting and tweeting, stretching what was essentially one good joke very thinly indeed. Quickly, large swathes of Twitter are sick to death of them. Within two weeks most people find an RT of @shitdonaldtrump as droll as hearing the *Spitting Image* 'Chicken Song' for the 3,457th time since 1982.

Within a week of @shitdonaldtrump's birth the parody tweeter (or tweeters, as there is often more than one person running the account) is frustrated they can't reveal their true self as they are clearly such a great writer/ humorist/marketeer. They are contacting publishing houses pitching to make @shitdonaldtrump into a book and contacting broadsheet newspapers to offer articles on 'The face behind the tweet', 'How I came up with my great @shitdonaldtrump idea' or simply 'How I write' (having written a whopping 700 words in total).

Occasionally a small publishing house whipped up in a 'Stick Your Buzz Up Your Azz'-style Twitter marketing whirlwind will sign the tweeter, not really understanding what the book is but knowing there are enough easily pleased readers in Britain to make a book by Aleksandr Meerkat – a novel penned by someone pretending to be a meerkat from a compare-insurance website advert - a soaraway literary hit.

If the celebrity who is being lampooned is on Twitter, they will have this site pointed out to them 100 times a minute in their @ mentions column, every time they log on. Eventually they'll respond claiming they find it 'really funny' and 'the highest tribute', all natural emotions felt, obviously, when being publicly ridiculed.

8. Things to do lists

bobbitybong Homebase for 40 watt light bulbs and emulsion Rock n roll.

KarenCapers Need box files for new tax return. Can't face Staples.

Lizzietish Hector for coffee. Bank at 11am. Squash with Paula. Parents evening. Never stops.

These sort of mundane life-chores should really be confined to a page on a rough note jotter, headed off with a big, purposefully scrawled THINGS TO DO and with doodles of pictures of cats on skateboards around the margins of the page which you added while taking a phone call from your mother.

A proper old-school To Do list is a thing of great beauty. The author can return after every finished task and sweep a line through its reminder with a proud accomplished DONE. Finishing such a list is a chronicle of a day well spent. So why are people posting their lists of errands on Twitter? Unwalked dogs, unbooked dentist appointments, unbought milk, unfiled expense claims – they litter the timeline, hanging round in the collective subconscious, cluttering cyberspace with unfinished business FOREVER. You could read Twitter on a beach in Mustique sipping a rum cooler and come away feeling subconsciously angsty about @josiedrivel's ongoing fight with Amazon.com about a missing child's swingball set.

9. Food anxiety tweets

Dollydaydream There were three bagels in the cup-board and now there is one. Oh dear!

OMG, Dolly, you've eaten two bagels? You only meant to eat one, right? That's got to be, like, 700 calories. And you only meant to allow yourself 350 for lunch. You must feel like a real pig. How, Dolly, how did you end up eating two bagels? You'll no doubt end up eating the third one now over the space of the next few days. That's so like you. This is classic Dolly. This is like your tweet yesterday when you ate a bag of pretzels on top of your couscous-salad lunch. Or the day before when you ate a whole slice of birthday cake even though you had complex carbs at dinner. Thank god Twitter is here so slim people can broadcast all these riveting examples of eating slightly more than they planned to eat, which makes no odds as the rest of the time they eat slightly less than everyone else. This shit is dynamite. You should put this in a blog, then make people pay to subscribe.

10. I'm-on-drugs tweets

davethedad Big up old skool chicago house vibez! byron stingily IS THE DON, Tuuneage!

Ten minutes later:

davethedad Whistle posseeee can I hear you?

Ten minutes later:

davethedad Big up all the wigan ravers!

Ten minutes later:

davethedad WOOT WOOT ENERGY!!!

As a general rule of thumb, anyone tweeting 'WOOT WOOT ENERGY!!!' at 3am in the morning tends to be high on pharmaceuticals and not doing anything at all which would remotely use up 'energy'. In @davethedad's mind he is DJing to a rowdy lunchtime afterparty in DC10 in Ibiza. In actual fact @davethedad is at his kitchen table in Cleethorpes finishing off the rest of some shocking quality cocaine and posting links to old acid-house records on YouTube, while his wife sleeps with a pillow over her head, mentally dividing up all their assets.

Over the course of the evening @davethedad's tweets will become markedly less coherent and/or more sexual, eventually resulting at 6am in terrible droning Velvet Underground or Terence Trent D'Arby ballads which he will announce as 'WOOT. Totally balleric'.

(Warning: tweeting @davethedad back will only encourage him.)

On the other hand, celebrities on drugs on Twitter is a spectacular combo. Five in the morning with a belly full of Vicodin is precisely when a celebrity looks at his/her follower count (5 million), realises their highly paid public-relations guru is probably asleep, and thinks this would be a great chance to break free of all this 'media-constructed-image bullshit' and show the world 'the real them'. American rappers are particularly splendid at filling everyone's Twitter timeline up with unadulterated cocaine brain-fart, rambling on and on until whatever time their assistant is alerted. On getting the panicked call from a record-company minion, the assistant will drive herself at full speed to their mansion, knock the rapper to the floor like an England rugby prop, then lock herself in a laundry cupboard with all of his iPhones, laptops and chargers.

11. I-won't-be-here-for-a-while tweets

Drabdarren Just to say I won't be here for a while as I'm getting on a train with bad reception.

Oh, phew, Darren, cheers for keeping us in the loop, bruv. Man, if you'd not tweeted for half an hour, we'd have been pressing that refresh button in a right old state, then nagging the police to send out a dog pack. Daz, just for future reference – how long do you guesstimate you might leave between tweets from now on? Just so we can tell if you're eating lunch or writing a report, and haven't fallen down a massive pit behind the photocopier and are in need of emergency rescue. Three minutes? Five minutes? More? TELL US, DARREN, WE MUST KNOW.

josiedrivel Going to holiday cottage for 4 days. Will try to tweet.

Woah woah woah, Josie! Hang on there, sweetcheeks. You're going to be gone for four days and you'll TRY to tweet? Trying isn't good enough. We need commitment. Me and you, we're in this for the long haul. You know the rules around here. It's all very good being a 'name' on Twitter, slinging your thoughts and bons mots around harum-scarum, being the toast of the timeline, but the moment we stop tweeting, Josie, we don't exist. GONE. FORGOTTEN. So we can never, never stop tweeting, Josie. Never. We're like sharks. We've got to keep swimming or we die.

12. Brainrot bargain-basement section

Carrycargo HOORAY!! I've just made 2,000 follow-ers.

josiedrivel woohoo 10,000 followers. That's like a small village!

This is a great way to alienate and rankle those with less followers and prompt others to unfollow you through sheer pettiness.

Billybabble OMG I missed my 3000 post. I was going to dedicate it but now I'm on 3007. *celebrates in hindsight*

Billy, I could actually slap you in the face for robbing me of that two seconds.

Upsetursula Please RT to raise awareness of Blue Waffle Fanny Malady.

Dear Ursula, NO. I've Googled this illness and it's fucking disgusting. I'm not bumming everyone else out.

> **Kevinkrud** @twitlonger I am cycling across the Alp for Poorly Kittens Charity. The flight/accom cost £3,000. I need to make £1,600 in sponsorship to justify going on this really amazing trip. Please RT, despite getting about 100 of these an hour and me not even following you.

BLOCK.

The terrible
oh why have you unfollowed
me email of doom

Dear @gracedent,

I have just received a prompt from Qwitter informing me I've been unfollowed by you. Why is this? I hope you don't find this email awkward and intrusive to receive, but I would really appreciate an answer about this, as I am gravely wounded and think I deserve to know why you would be so careless and slipshod with my emotions. I've just this moment got off the telephone to my therapist about this and she completely agreed – eventually, in a roundabout sense – that it would be best if I tackled you head-on.

Yours, @helgaharangue

GRACEBOT 3.0 AUTOMATED RESPONSE

Thankyou @helgaharangue for your recent enquiry. Before

we process your request, please avail yourself of @grace-dent's list of top ten potential reasons you have been unfollowed which may make further action unnecessary.

1. You're the sort of masochistic whiner who uses Qwitter . . .

Or Unfollowr. Or Lostafollower.com Or @goodbye-buddy – and then dispatches emails right away. Plain and simple. Why would you do this to yourself? Years ago, I used to go to school with a boy who would come into school some mornings and write, 'Who doesn't like me?' across the board with chalk and then push the chalk in-to our hands for us to tick or cross. This boy also liked to (a) get up on to the school roof and throw tiles at teach-ers and (b) set fire to stuff.

There is something quite off-putting about people who want extra pain in their life. People who read the news-paper and see mass rape in Darfur, genital mutilation in Uganda, earthquake orphans in Pakistan, fizzing nuclear reactors in Japan, Richard Dawkins telling us there's no point praying as there never was a god, and Stephen Hawking telling us we're on the last legs of the end of the world, and then think, 'Oh this is all so depressing.

I think I'll go and check my unfollow software and then sit in a room dwelling over who pressed a button to say they didn't like me today.'

You Qwitter users are basically the emo-rock corner of Twitter, sat in your bedrooms peeping from under your slightly too long crimped fringes, listening to Funeral For A Friend acoustic numbers, swigging small amounts of Domestos cream bleach, then checking your unfollow count. In essence, you were unfollowed because you're a bit annoying right now. And the fact you then found out and are annoying people to tell you why you're annoying is really annoying. Stop being annoying.

2. Too much tweeting

From your cheery 'greetings!' at 7am, to the twitpic of your first coffee, to an anecdote about your postman arriving, to a rumination on the hard skin on your feet that needs pumicing, to your forays into finding your car keys, to your observations on whether you're tired or not tired today, to your not-even-remotely-amusing story about taking the wrong file to work, to your totally-not-even-an-anecdote-just-shit-that-is-passing-through-your-frontal-cortex about 'whether to have a coffee on the way to work or at work and save £2 at Starbucks'

OH MY GOD. STOP TWEETING. NO-ONE, NOT EVEN YOUR OWN MOTHER, IS THIS INTERESTED IN THIS LEVEL OF DETAIL. SERIOUSLY, TRY CALLING HER UP AND TELLING HER THIS SHIT AND SEE HOW LONG SHE ENDURES YOU BEFORE SHE TURNS UP THE VOLUME ON *WATERCOLOUR CHALLENGE* AND STOPS PICKING UP. You know when a toddler first learns to speak and form sentences and they begin a constant, neverending commentary on life – 'Moon!' 'Fire engine!' 'Train' – which everyone has to respond to with, 'Yes, moon! Yes, fire engine!'? That's you on Twitter. Well, it was – I don't follow you any more.

3. You overused your DM option

The direct-message facility is a wondrous, highly intimate way of communicating. It allows you to add a secret, funny/snarky meta-conversation to the public conversation that's happening in the timeline. It allows you to say things privately to a tweeter that you might not want broadcast and to form closer bonds. It gives you access to someone who doesn't afford it to just anyone. Have you been abusing this privilege? Did you immediately begin bombarding them with messages asking 'how they are?'

every time they appeared? Did you use DM to demand an RT for your cause/blog? Did you offer to send the tweeter something which roughly related to something they mentioned on their timeline and then ask them again and again, then dispatch the gift and then begin DMing to ask what they thought of it?

Did you stop communicating in the timeline with the tweeter, as why would you need to since you now have a fast-track way of getting them on DM? Well, this is why you got quietly unfollowed. Tweeters don't want their DM box to be just an extension of their work email in-box, full of nagging requests to respond to things. The easiest way to stop this is to unfollow you.

4. We have nothing in common. NOTHING

You are a perfectly pleasant individual, but we couldn't be more opposite if a lab had created us. And not in a sexy, hair-pulling 'opposites attract, look at our two big sexy brains bashing together' sort of way either. That would be amazing. No, we just have no common ground at all. I'm not even sure how the hell I ended up following you. I can only imagine at one point there was a bizarre blip in Earth's natural order and for that millisecond we were compatible. But that moment burned bright and fast. And now it turns out you like 'training for Iron Man tournament' (and updating on how much liquid and sugar you've taken on today), and making trouble at your local Parent–Teacher Group about the ongoing parallel-parking dilemma near the Sprocket Roundabout. You like parroting various Conservative Party thinktank views on 'social mobility'. Oh, and you don't own a television. WTF is all that about? I can't get my head around that. In fact, I find anyone who doesn't own a TV sinister. I can only imagine you use all this extra time when I'm lying splayed on a beanbag watching *Pets Win Prizes* or *Big Brother* to plot some sort of macabre world domination. Sadly the only interesting tweets you'd muster up while annexing France for crazy despot purposes would be how many calories are in a croque-monsieur. Bore off.

5. You RT praise about yourself

Oh lordy me, I wish this didn't annoy me so much because it would improve my time on Twitter. And, yes, I completely accept that Twitter is a way for people to market their wares and, yes, I agree that we all have to keep the wolf from the door and feather our own nests. And, yes, I believe that a little smattering of 'This is what

I am proud to be up to this week' here and there is the bread and butter of Twitter.com. BUT as the great philosopher Chas from the up-tempo boogie-woogie pub-blues combo Chas & Dave says in the song 'Rabbit': 'With your excessive talking, you're becoming a pest.'

Do you have any real grip on how conversation works in real life? Is it like this?

Me: Hello, Helga Harangue, how are you today?

Helga: I'm good, Grace, because Steven in Lincolnshire says I am one of the most compelling conversationalists ever.

Me: Oh. That's nice.

Helga: YES, and Sally says that my article in the *Gazette* today challenged her preconceptions about soap-based face washes and also made her laugh out loud.

Me: Oh, OK. (*Begins to check watch and invent fanciful getaway lie.*)

Helga: Oh, and Clark in Consett says that I am a unique and respected voice and everyone should listen to me.

Me: That's great, Helga, I must rush now as I've promised to crochet a small cardigan for a maverick woodland badger using my garden as a base for *Wind in the Willows*-style adventures. Bye.

Everyone has to bring something to the party on Twitter, and the only thing you bring is news of yourself. I will follow anyone at all I can chat to. And anyone who makes me laugh. And although I do find your ego amusing to a certain point, it's a sort of Joe Pesci 'amusing' that could go wrong at any point and make me very hulky-smash-smash, and that's not good.

6. You @ people's names in on abusive/critical/trolling messages

If you think it's OK to write unpleasant things about people like this:

> Has @julielotterylady put on weight? She looks like a pig in that dress tonight.

and @ in the name of the person you're talking about, well, I don't want to be friends with you.

Call it self-preservation, but I'm sensing you're a nasty piece of work. @-bombing people's mentions column with 'Shit you're saying to everyone else about them, but in the third person, directly to their face' is the action of a buttwipe. Not only will the person see this right away – and, believe me, they will see it: even at 100k followers you see almost every @mention, they don't pass so quickly – they will also see every subsequent mention of the insult by a flurry of their friends who RT the tweet, and by all the people who reply to your tweet and leave the @name in too.

Perhaps this level of rudeness is excusable if the person you're @-bombing is the head of Evil Manufacturers Inc exploiting poor Africans, but, hang on, this is just Julie who pulls out the National Lottery balls on the Wednesday-night TV show. Does Julie need to read 52 different @mentions of her being a fat pig while in the taxi home? Just because you're using Twitter, is being a horrible jerk acceptable? If Julie worked in your office would you perch yourself on the end of her desk at work, with your back to her, facing the rest of the staff, and shout: 'I THINK JULIE IS A MASSIVE FAT COW' and then calmly sit down and ask, 'What? What have I done? I was only saying she was fat. I didn't think she'd hear it!? Bloody hell, she needs to be a bit thicker-skinned about things'?

Be catty if you want – Twitter lives and breathes by it – but @-bombing a name means you actually want the person to be hurt. And if you do want people to be hurt, then please don't get all pissy and theatrical when the person replies to you in an equally mean manner. The general rule is this: people who @-bomb names in on abuse messages are almost always the people who become the most hysterical when an equally harsh message comes whizzing back. They will immediately RT this 'unwarranted abuse' and spend days bleating about their hurt feelings and assessing whether the abuse they sent warranted the terrible insult they received. Grow up.

7. You were a friend of a friend of a friend . . .

. . . And by following the full set of your clique, my timeline is pretty much swamped with all of you using Twitter instead of direct message or instant messaging, round the clock. Now, this is brilliant if I'm in the mood for all of you, and you, well, you seem lovely, I like you, but I've trimmed your clique down to two or three of the least verbose members now. And, believe me, they're more than happy to keep voyeurs fully informed of your news. If I want to know what's happening with your life, I can just press 'see conversation' on TweetDeck and enjoy this extended dissection of whether the restaurant you've all booked for Friday night caters for wheat-intolerants.

8. You're a stuck fucking record

I used to really enjoy following you, but of late you've got a bee in your bonnet about an issue and you won't shut up about it. Are you the person who wants a local MP to resign? Or the one who doesn't want a Nando's in your high street? Or are you the person who finds the third verse of 'Three Blind Mice' homophobic? Or the woman campaigning to have sugar taken out of jam so it's not even jam it's just fucking squashed fruit but at least diabetics and babies can eat it? Oh, hang on! You're the woman who wants your toddler's carol service moved to a bigger venue as no-one can get tickets for their nannies! How could I forget. You started off with a few narky tweets about this, but now it's become 'a campaign' with a hashtag! And you're updating everyone about every item of correspondence with the school and argument with the headmistress (who, frankly, I feel sorry for. In fact, I'M ON HER SIDE). And when people hint playfully that you're being a bit repetitive, you go into hyperdrive and start squawking that you're enjoying LOTS OF BRILLIANT FEEDBACK about your campaign. Which you are, off the two other people with the same tedious hobby-horse issue as you. And I've tried to stay patient and interested but I've failed, so you've been unfollowed. I'll follow you again when you've gone back to normal. It's just Twitter, don't sweat it.

9. You have offended me in real life

You have become somewhat of a douche in real life, and I'm sure this will pass, but while your social skills are failing their MOT I've decided to unfollow. The fact you can pull it together to be a 'really nice person' on Twitter while not tackling the virulent social mess you cause 'IRL' makes me hivey. You could have caused any number of crimes. Are you happily twatting on in my timeline yet won't commit to any email asking whether you're attending the dinner we're having this weekend? Are you completely untrustworthy with a secret and can't stop blabbing? Does having all eyes on you hanging on your every salacious word give you a sharp thrill? Have you revealed yourself as a consummate backstabber? Did you not show up for a dual presentation last week and then tweet you were having your eyelashes extended? Did you grab the first taxi in the street at 3am, leaving me alone at kicking-out time in Soho with a load of drunks and crackheads? Do you treat everyone like lucky competition winners allowed the gift of some face-time? Are you a continuous adulterer and we all have to watch you buttering up your next victim? Have you become a douche?

You are unfollowed. I love you to pieces. Call me when you're better.

10. I don't even remember unfollowing you. I was drunk

Oh dear. You may have been pruned during a point when I was very inebriated and with the 20/20 clarity of drunkenness I thought: 'Jesus Christ, who ARE all thesh people quacking on about rubbish? Oh, Twitter is totally stupid. I don't even speak to these people or know them but they're ALL IN MY HEAD. I don't NEED any extra people in my head! Hey, wouldn't it be really neat if I, like, followed hardly anyone? I'd just be like this totally mysterious enigmatic voice who followed, say, 20 people and even then only made REALLY COOL, controlled responses to them, like David Bowie would be if he was on Twitter . . . Yeah, now I think I AM a lot like David Bowie, oh Ziggggggy, Zigggy played giiitar [*swigs amaretto out of the bottle*]. Yeah, that's right, I'm unfollowing everyone, YOU and YOU and YOU . . . I donsh need this type of head interference in my life, I am a WRITER. An artisht of words, and Twitter is inhibiting me from creating really life-affirming literature. Screw all of you. UNFOLLOW!'

On reflection, this was a bit rash. I'm a bit embarrassed. Let's say no more about this, I'm following you again.

You have been watching . . .

We're a diverse bunch in Twitterland, but no timeline is complete without these main cast members:

@WilfWang *Naturally funny man*

Twitter, en masse, adores @WilfWang. He's genuinely very funny. Wilf's a trusted source for RT-tastic links, wry satirical swipes and rapid-response one-liners. Remember when Osama died? What about Wilf's royal wedding coverage? He frickin' nailed it. Wilf isn't a professional comedian, he's a part-time uni lecturer/struggling graphic artist/occasional listings writer/sporadic blogger and provincial pub thinker, but his tweets are the meat and bones of this godforsaken place. Wilf is adored by male tweeters, and women have studied his avatar, think he needs a restyle and a bit of TLC but after that they'd definitely give him one.

Although Wilf has a 200% higher daily 'LOLZ' output

than Ollie Droll, millionaire comedian (see below), he is flat broke as he's got no head for business and gives all his brain power away for free. Several famous comedians follow @WilfWang, and he suspects they are stealing his jokes but is too polite to say and he still hopes one day he will infiltrate their gang and be a writer. Wilf will be side-splittingly on-form in an esoteric, zingy, clever way for five days in a row, then go AWOL, for days, which he'll claim was down to a cold but was actually due to chronic depression.

@ConstanceRimmer *Consummate career climber*

Never before has the brown-tongued path to career advancement been as transparent. For @ConstanceRimmer, cosying up to people who can whisk her up life's ladder is a 24/7 job. Constance's timeline gurgles with fake ROFLs, strategically placed RTs and faux-concern about other tweeters' lives. She is the Queen of Inveiglement, her true forte being to hone in on important/well-known newbies at that vulnerable 'Twitter Beginner' stage like a big sister helping them settle in (translation: groom them as a contact).

This involves:

(a) Introducing the new tweeter's username to all her own followers with a big, over-the-top fanfare. This draws the newcomer's attention to Constance's account and also works as a sort of Twitter territorial cyber-pissing ritual: 'I CLAIM THIS SCALP!'

(b) Sending a public tweet to the newbie informing them they are 'a real role model'.

(c) Tweeting and tweeting and tweeting and tweeting the person every time they speak in the manner of a chummy confidante.

(d) Eventually being followed, only to begin DMing the person with requests for an address where she can send a muffin basket.

What's that, Constance? It's someone important's daughter's birthday this week? You need to be all over that like a frickin' Navy SEAL:

> **ConstanceRimmer** @bigbosskate How did Amelia's 4th birthday go!?
>
> **ConstanceRimmer** @bigbosskate Did those fairy-lights I told you about arrive!?
>
> **ConstanceRimmer** @bigbosskate Oh bless! She loved them! So good to hear!

ConstanceRimmer @bigbosskate Big hugs to Little miss Amelia.

At 2am, while you're eating cheese and crackers and watching *Jonathan Creek* re-runs, @ConstanceRimmer is on Twitter publicly thanking your CEO for the 'really great chat over cocktails' which 'totally inspired her'. You try not to mind Constance but you hope she means the CEO 'inspired her to shoot herself in the head with a whale harpoon'.

@olliedroll *Millionaire comedian*

@olliedroll is colossally famous. Ollie knows exactly how to make money out of being funny and it doesn't involve tweeting LOLZ to the public for free. To be frank, @olliedroll can't see the pissing point of Twitter at all. He doesn't want to speak to anyone; in fact, he only joined because his agent warned him people were impersonating him, and he wasn't standing for that. Despite Ollie's timeline being as funny as heavy-flow menstruation on a beach holiday, he has amassed more than 500,000 followers, whom he thrills bi-weekly with links to tour dates and nods to serious broadsheet opinion pieces which we're all grateful he's slung his powerhouse brain behind. Ollie works with a group of trusted gag writers and has no qualms about parroting their jokes – formed from reconstituted parts of @WilfWang's Twitter feed – as his own on panel shows.

Despite @olliedroll's wealth and fame he is never remotely happy. Ollie thinks he outgrew 'all this shit' years ago and that he should be in Hollywood working for HBO with Larry David and Jerry Seinfeld. Ollie doesn't tweet that, but then he doesn't really have to.

@CassandraCoy *Dream woman*

Cassie works very hard on Twitter to seem like the perfect woman. Cassie – or at least the version of Cassie which she puts over in her timeline – is a solid reminder to married men of how life used to be with their wife before real life took over and the house began to smell of Napisan and damp cat litter and the only conversations became about recycling boxes. Cassie's avatar is a coquettish headshot of her in full make-up, sporting a professional blow dry and looking fragrant and foxy at a wedding reception. Her timeline is essentially just a row of signifiers, styled as intricately as a *Living Etc* shoot, saying, 'You'd be much better off with me. I am deeply into cult TV, art, fringe comedy, indie music; I'm a real nerd like you deep down – ssssh, don't tell anyone. I love getting tipsy on fine wines and conversations about Proust and I'm terribly upfront about sex.'

CassandraCoy OMG @olliedroll. New Bob Dylan box set!!! Wow, going to listen to it while I take a hot shower. Happyface.

CassandraCoy Oh @WilfWang. We must have a long lunch and chat about The Cure.

One thing Cassie is never upfront about is her husband. Cassie is married to some hapless idiot who doesn't understand Twitter, and she sure as hell isn't encouraging him. Cassie does occasionally play the 'I have children' card as this gives her further leverage with @olliedroll, @WilfWang and @dylandilf for cosy DM chats about Calpol and much more.

@dylandilf *Slightly lost stay-at-home dad*

Dylan has been up since 5am with a toddler. He isn't dressed, his armpits smell cheesy and he's watched the same *Peppa Pig* DVD three times through a sleep-deprived haze. Dylan is hungry and thirsty but he does not dare go into the kitchen and make a coffee as his child is going through a stage of barging in, pulling a chair to the work surface yelling, 'ME MAKE OMELETTE!!' 77 times in a row, and, when he refuses, rolling around screaming until her cheeks go scarlet, then pale green. This seems like a lot of grief, so Dylan is just going to sit on the floor surrounded by all the plastic foodstuffs from her My Little Kitchen and grab ten sneaky minutes on Twitter – his lifeline to the outside world – while the child fries imaginary eggs. Officially Dylan is supposed to be putting on a whites wash and sourcing good primary schools, but instead he's riffing with @WilfWang and flirting with @CassandraCoy and falling asleep on the floor when his daughter falls asleep and dreaming about slinging on some Bob Dylan and having sex in a hot shower with @CassandraCoy.

@therealsallysilkybuns A-list starlet

@therealsallysilkybuns is so tired of all this celebrity bullshit. The private jets to Cannes, the pre-red-carpet gown fittings, the post-fashion gala 'gifting suites' full of free Dolce & Gabbana, and those hellish dinner parties at Gwyneth Paltrow's house, shovelling down Gwynie's homemade three-bean guacamole perched between Jay-Z and that grumpy hippy from Coldplay. Sally is so supercrazy about Twitter as it gives her a chance to, y'know, just be real and totally connect with 'good people'. Sally's Twitter feed consists of:

(a) Twitpics of Sally's 'goofing about buddies' pulling faux-gang poses. On closer scrutiny these pictures aren't goofing about but 'Sally in a dressing room at work' and her 'buddies' are her make-up artist and stylist (i.e. people on her payroll).

(b) Assorted pictures of a small stupid-looking dog sitting in a $5k designer handbag, which begs the question: does it ever shit in there and would she even notice?

(c) Tweets airing Sally's grievances against the damned paparazzi for not giving her enough space at the airport today.

(d) Excruciatingly obvious corporate-sponsored ad tweets naming a mobile phone or a brand of pearls Sally 'can't live without!'

(e) Tweets praising whichever god, angel or spaceship controller she believes cosmically channelled her all that 'blessy' good fortune this week.

(f) Tweets gushing on about 'real people' she chanced upon this week who were 'so sweet' to her. 'OMG I Love you Cathay Pacific flight crew. You made me feel so at home!!!' Sally tweets, never quite realising that they upgraded her to seat number 1A and kissed her arse from JFK to Singapore because she is @therealsallysilkybuns.

@LeonardPhlegm *Self-styled misanthrope*

'I'm a very bad man,' Leonard warns in his bio. 'Do not follow, motherfuckers, if easily offended.' Leonard is single, white, male and in his late 20s or early 30s. Leonard's Twitter persona is a constantly vexed, toilet-humour-obsessed misanthrope. Leonard has amassed 900 followers, entranced by his tweets about 'big shits coming out of my bum' or 'sperm explosions from my cock!!' Leonard likes to make mean jokes about people who died one hour ago with a quick follow-up tweet of 'TOO SOON!!??' Poor Leonard is in a rut; he's sex-starved, neglected and needs some TLC. Career-wise, he would love to be a writer but lacks any real talent or net-working/social skills, which has given him a massive chip on his shoulder about the media being 'one big chummy, backslapping conspiracy' which he is bashing down BRICK BY BRICK by sitting behind his semen-encrusted Dell laptop tweeting female celebrities to point out he wouldn't have sex with them as 'YOU LOOK LIKE YOU HAVE A FAT VAGINA'. Leonard immediately RTs any upset replies asking to be left alone he gets from his victims, which Leonard's followers will lap up and RT again.

Leonard is hilarious if he's not picking on you. At the height of Leonard's trolling sprees, he will respond to being blocked by setting up new creepy faceless account after new creepy faceless account, especially to bombard a victim with one-liners. Eventually a nice girlfriend will come into Leonard's life and sort his head out, leaving him darkly ashamed about this stage in his life.

@garethglee *Teen queen*

Gareth is a young, recently out gay teenage boy from a provincial town. Gareth will hone in on you on Twitter after overhearing you discuss Rihanna's outfits, then he will follow you, then Follow Friday you, then tweet you ten times a day, LOLing at your jokes, then tweet messages in his timeline @ing your name saying that you're 'an inspiration' and his 'new Twitter BFF' and 'a god/goddess' and 'you should rule the world'. Then he will send you DMs asking if you can be his 'life mentor' and asking if you will read his blog and give feedback – your opinion would mean so much.

This continues for weeks until a point one night when he overhears another conversation you're having about

Rihanna's outfits which he is inexplicably angry about and begins tweeting that he is 'VERY LET DOWN' and you are a 'vile racialist homyphobe bitch', and eventually you have to block Gareth, pull the router out of the wall and hide under your bed.

@KelvinWebb *C-list celeb*

Kelvin has been 'in the public eye' for a decade. After winning Channel 5's *Don't Touch the Hutch*, Kelvin went on to present sob-story/home-improvement show *Boo-Hoo While We Build* on BBC1. Kelvin has 30,000 loyal followers whom he calls 'his guardian twangels'. He is eternally grateful to Twitter for keeping him emotionally afloat during his divorce from Sheena from GirlzUncut. Kelvin's timeline is:

(a) a collection of badly spelled grunts basically emoting what he can see in front of his eyes: 'Gd day today! Sun in sky innit! Alright my Twangels!!'

(b) RTs of messages from 'Twangels' saying, 'Gimme a RT shout out Kelvin! IT WOULD MEAN THE WORLD TO ME!!', which Kelvin does, making your timeline look like bad hospital radio.

(c) Tweets thanking everyone who came along to Dudley

to watch him presenting the *This Morning Wake Up to Weightloss Wack-a-mole Challenge!!*

(d) Teeth-gnashingly honest tweets after driving his kids back to their mother's mansion, which she took off him in the alimony settlement, then eating KFC alone in Scratchwood Services forecourt.

@alanapoplectic *Livid political activist*

Alan is from a nice middle-class family, attended a good university, has travelled extensively and is in steady work but is still FUCKING LIVID ABOUT THIS GODFORSAKEN WORLD. Alan likes to lurk around Twitter, listening to other people's conversations, before DRAGGING them round to one of his tub-thumping specialist subjects. Oh, you've bought a pie for dinner to-night, have you? Well, Alan hopes you enjoy that pie, knowing that THE SUPERMARKET HAS LINKS WITH FISHERMEN WHO BREAK EU RULINGS ON HERRING TRAWLING IN NORWAY! You do not want to anger angry Alan with your use of a misogynistic pronoun or slightly outdated, totally innocuous slang word which he has recently decided is sexist, homophobic or islamophobic because Alan will RT you and inflame the attention of Twitter's 'dudes in a moral panic' twitchfork squad and you, my friend, are shafted. (See also Alan's cousin, *Single-issue hobbyhorse Cynthia*. Cynthia has a bee in her bonnet about one single topic: for example, 'the representation in the media of women who own tortoises'. She has a TweetDeck column open searching for the word 'tortoise' and she sits like Cato awaiting Inspector Clouseau, waiting for someone in the world to mention the word so she can start screaming she is reporting them to 'the authorities'.)

@borisboom3_2 *Hip kid*

Boris only comes on Twitter to laugh at 'retards' and post links to his LIVE dubstep/cockcore/fartgasm u-stream show coming to your screen from a boiler-room in east London/Brooklyn. Sometimes Boris attends other DJs' nights, where he stands near the booth sporadically tweeting what's on the turntable, e.g. 'BANGING SMASH remix by cluckwang foo sounds BIG 2NIGHT.' Boris also tweets links to his blog, in which he reveals that he believes: (a) he'll be dead by the time he's 27; (b) that he and his chums invented the concept of taking drugs and staying out all night; and (c) the area he lives in is depressingly full of 'hipster scum' which he is not one of, despite moving from the sticks to that hip area as soon as he could as he was getting funny looks for insisting on wearing palazzo pants and a fez from the age of 11. On warm days Boris tweets pictures of him and his crew in the park surrounded by cheap screw-top wine bottles, bikes and miserable-looking, malnourished young women. All Boris's other tweets are twitpics of shit graffiti which Boris thinks is 'coleslawsome'. He doesn't realise that in 20 years' time he will be part of a Neighbourhood Watch scheme to prosecute kids for doing exactly that.

@tinatitsoot *Sex worker*

Tina is a chatty, jolly type who you can't help but warm to. Tina is also an escort/adult-movie star/'big beautiful woman' who 'hosts parties'/one of those deluded teenage students who believes writing a Belle-de-Jour-esque blog documenting the ins and outs of her knickers for middle-aged men to pant over makes her a fourth-wave feminist. You like Tina a lot; but it's tricky having her in your timeline, what with Tina's avatar being her bent over a desk naked, with an orange in her mouth, and her bio being a link to a blog warbling on about 'WHY bukkake parties should not be maligned as wrong', which you don't actually hold ANY opinion on other than 'TINA, PLEASE STOP TALKING ABOUT YOUR FANNY'.

@victorvaguelypissy *The passive-aggressive prodder*

Victor is following you for some odd reason, because although he is never rude or confrontational, like a death of a thousand paper cuts he wants you to know he's not keen on you. Victor will respond to your cheery, observational tweets with small barbed responses like 'Jealous much?' or 'Yawn' or by suddenly becoming French ('A slightly cute argument, non?' or 'More mindrot, n'est-ce pas?') or Elizabethan ('You tweet too much, methinks'). Victor will carry on in this manner, being not exactly rude but certainly not friendly, until you are sick of the sight of him and block him, whence he will dispatch 'the terrible oh why have you unfollowed me boo-hoo hissyfit email of doom' and be genuinely sad and mystified you had to let him go.

@SamCram *Secretly very boring man*

Sam has a funny avatar and a witty bio and tweets prolifically and he follows all your favourite funniest tweeters and woo-hoo this is going to be SO GREAT you're so glad you found him . . . so you follow him for four months and . . . NOTHING. Bugger all. No amusing links. No great one-liners. No news. No views. Just weird sub-*Withnail and I* yadder such as 'Morning! I demand breakfast and I demand it now!' or 'Aaagh! icy carpark – curse ye gods!!' or 'Missed the bus again – damn you mr 27 busdriver!'

Sam adds absolutely nothing to Twitter except background white noise, and one day you realise your brain RAM is being used up by him while you forget about your own niece's birthday, so you quietly cull him and feel quite bad.

@Peter101 *Twitter busybody*

As dour-faced pop god Morrissey once said, 'There's always someone, somewhere, with a big nose, who knows' – which foresaw Twitter's Peter Pedant. Peter gains deep joy from swooping down in the midst of throwaway conversations and fucking the fun times up with annoying corrections.

josiedrivel omg! have you seen Lindsay Lohan's new hair disaster??

SallyStarlight ugh. I am so disinterested in Lohan's hot mess look right now.

168

Peter101 'Disinterested' isn't 'uninterested'. A disinterested person is aware but impartial, an uninterested person doesn't care about the subject.

josiedrivel wtf?

Or:

Mandymoonbeam Customer services at Amazing Shoes are totally ignoring me. Don't want to escalate the matter.

Karencupcake You need to say something Mandy – you've been waiting indoors for those shoes for days.

Peter101 Escalators go down as often as they go up, so the verb 'to escalate' is utterly meaningless.

Mandymoonbeam oh piss off peter.

Peter is physically unable to stop being a pedantic douche, even though he knows it wins him no friends. When challenged on Twitter over why he's being so picky, Peter will immediately wilt like an overwatered spider plant muttering that 'he doesn't mumph know, it's just a thing he mumph does'. When Peter isn't lurking around Twitter waging war against wrongness, he's working unpaid for Wikipedia, bashing the 'clarification needed here' button or cluttering up online news-comment threads with 'less vs fewer' narks and getting very het up about wonky uses of the third conditional tense. Last Christmas Peter spent the day on his own roaming Twitter, pointing out that Christmas should be capitalised, before telephoning the number on the back of the can of Heinz sausages in beans he had for lunch to point out a split infinitive on the back-of-the-can blurb.

@ianfantile *Is-that-a-euphemism man*

Marymooch1 Why are Ikea shelves so impossible to screw in?

DavyCr0cket_ I know. You need a sonic screwdriver and an arm like Hagar.

ianfantile IS THAT A EUPHEMISM!!!??

DavyCr0cket_ Did you vote today in the local election?

gracedent my polling station today was completely empty.

ianfantile IS THAT SOME KIND OF EUPHEMISM??

Is that a euphemism?!! That MUST be a euphemism! Ian's mind is so finely tuned to reading coded symbols for vaginal penetration/massive breasts that his world outlook is very limited. Ian has been advised by medical professionals not to log on to Twitter during popular BBC show *The Great British Bake Off* as the overload of tweets about 'cream horns', 'floury baps', 'iced slices' and 'sticky fancies' lead to him actually hyperventilating with double-entendre-induced mirth and needing to be placed in a darkened room with a chilled tea towel on his face.

@garygetaroom *Twitter cockblock*

Gary scours Twitter for anyone having a nice chat with anyone else of the opposite sex so he can bellow, 'GET A ROOM YOU GUYS!!' with slack-jawed glee. Gary is the ultimate internet knobhead, stamping on the delicate pitter-patter of two tweeters coquettishly busting each other's chops or discussing rare Shins B-sides or simply talking about the weather by barging in banging a big bass drum and basically hooting 'WOOOOOOOH HOOOOO! LOOK AT THESE TWO FLIRTING WITH EACH OTHER! THEY ARE SO KISSING UP A TREE. K.I.S.S.I.N.G.! There is a special place in hell for @garygetaroom, not that he'll notice as he'll be listening to Satan's goblins chatting about rotas and shouting, 'WOAH YOU GUYS NEED TO GET A ROOM!'

@karen_drab *Undercover hotty*

Nobody listened to a single damned solitary word @karen_drab said during the 17 months that her avatar was a ginger cat asleep on a rocking chair with a twibbon saying 'Save the New Forests'. But then one day Karen changed her avatar to a personal headshot and she just happens to look like Natalie Portman and something peculiar happened: suddenly her opinions have become MUCH MUCH more valid and boys all over Twitter are suddenly fascinated by her views on *Question Time*, *Doctor Who* and electoral reform, and whether or not if they keep chipping away and being totally fascinated by her she'll eventually let her do it to them.

@billyboohoo *Spoiler baby*

Billy hasn't really got his brain around the concept of 'the worldwide web'. 'I'm on the bus home from work so NO GLEE SPOILERS please,' he harangues Twitter. 'OMG I'm in Lanzarote until Monday, CAN EVERYONE NOT TWEET ABOUT MASTERCHEF?' he moans at 200 million people. 'I'm on night shifts right through June, so NO-ONE TALK ABOUT EASTENDERS,' he says, while simultaneously standing by the sea compelling it not to wash against Brighton. 'OMG I've got 5 more seasons of Sopranos on box set to watch – NO SPOILERZ,' he demands, decreeing that no-one on earth mentions one of the most culturally important TV shows ever made as he's not quite got round to updating his Amazon order. 'I JUST THINK IF YOU HAD ANY RESPECT YOU'D THINK ABOUT ME, M'KAY,' he shouts, as Twitter gives him a wedgie and then chucks his schoolbag in the pond.

@s27wighorn345 *Silent, invisible lurker*

'Hi, Julie,' a vague acquaintance says at your child's school's parent evening. 'How's the new fence?'

'Erm, it's, erm . . . fine . . . How do you know about the fence?' you say.

'Oh, you were talking about it to Pippa.'

Your mind races. Who is Pippa?

'So did you get those Blur tickets in the end?' she asks. Now you're freaked out.

'Errrr, yes, how did you know I wanted Blur tickets?'

'Oh, you were talking about it with Paul,' she says.

'Paul? When was I talking about that? Hang on, are you on Twitter?'

'Oh, no. I'm not on Twitter, really, I just go on there. I have an account but I never post. I just watch you all. It's such fun.'

Celebrities on Twitter

Celebrities certainly don't provide the pithiest tweets, the funniest links or the cleverest thoughts on Twitter, but hot damn, you'd be forgiven for thinking they DO. Celebs on Twitter, just like in their real pampered lives, well, they're kind of a big deal. Celebs' mediocre ramblings get retweeted to high heaven, their half-formed 140-character brainfarts are cut, pasted and reported on news sites as *The News*, their follower counts grow like Japanese knotweed even when they're not saying anything, and, most aggravating of all, when they do tweet, they seem to be in a special 'We're Famous' sect and only want to tweet to each other. What's that all about? I've spoken to many famouses and this is what I've worked out . . .

Frequently asked questions

Q. Why do celebs love Twitter?

A. A mix of these five reasons:

(i) They don't think they're famous ENOUGH yet. Deep down, few celebrities truly believe their publicity department is focused enough on telling the planet how brilliant they are. Now they can do it themselves.

(ii) Twitter is an instant high. Being famous has many 'ups': fancy cars picking you up, free Nando's chicken vouchers, everyone wanting to shag you. And many lows: being photographed in the *Daily Mail* online 'Sidebar of Shame' picking your thong out of your bumcrack outside Starbucks, accompanied by a story saying you've gained ten pounds. During the bad times the celeb can reach into their pocket, tap their Twitter app and get a cyber-cuddle from 12,000 fans. It feels so gooooood.

(iii) A rising follower count is 'progress'. It's something seemingly solid they can take strength from.

(iv) They need to look youthful and relevant to get bookings, and not like the weird technophobe dinosaur still asking their agent to update their Myspace.

(v) If they don't join, well, Mr A. Weirdo sitting at home in Huddersfield will open an account and pretend to be them and begin charming their fans and issuing statements on their behalf.

Q. But why are celebs all such matey chummy backslappy showbiz pals with each other? It's like a secret club.

A. If you follow lots of celebs, their lovey, over-the-top intra-celeb burble will take over your screen. Annoying? Perhaps. But you are following a set of friends, like any other clique of friends, and they are using Twitter exactly like you do, to stay in contact, make plans for beers, take the piss out of each other and send messages of support. The showbiz circuit is just like working in any other large corporate firm with a hundred different departments: people get to know each other. Take the London 'celebrity circuit', for example. It's actually minuscule, consisting essentially of a few West End theatres, a few major TV channel headquarters, some private members' clubs (posh pubs), some agents' offices and the *This Morning* sofa with Pip and Holly. Day after day, celebs pinball around London, bashing into each other, killing time in make-up rooms, working on projects, meeting on school runs and being invited to the same dinner parties. Of course they're going to follow each other on Twitter, then use it to stay in touch. Following hundreds of celebrities on Twitter and then whining that 'they all know each other' is a bit like logging on to the Liverpool FC fan forum and complaining that the people in the 'Season Ticket' thread are cliquey and all have a backstory.

Q. But why don't they just talk privately? They know we can hear, right?

A. Believe it or not, they ARE talking privately on direct message, too. Celebs very often use Twitter just to touch base, then switch to another more private platform to speak privately; thus the part you read where they're burbling on in eye-watering detail to each other about their heavy menstruation, their ingrown toenail and their bank-account overdraft is the part they don't mind you reading. Celebs tend to rethink this policy once they've seen details of their runny bowel movement written up on *E! Online* as a breaking-news bulletin.

Q. Why don't celebs reply to me?

A. Celebrities may have beautiful manicured hands and great biceps but they have the same number of fingers to work a phone as you do. Practically, they can't reply to everyone. Yes, if a famous tweeter with 100k followers sends a tweet and they're running their own Twitter from an app on their own mobile phone, then there is a strong chance they have read your reply, or at least scanned past it among hundreds of others in a millisecond, but tweeting back is often impossible. Celebs have the same sort of commitments as you do. Imagine walking into your nan's house for a natter and a cup of tea and saying: 'Sorry, Nan, no offence, but I just tweeted,

"How's your day?!" to 97,000 people on Twitter, and 2,257 just replied, so I need to go through my @ mentions and engage with everyone, and that will take, well, all day. I'll just sit here, don't bother me.' Would you do this, or would you politely hope your followers didn't expect individual replies? Also: when a celeb tweets an observation they often get the exact same 'play on words' or people deliberately misunderstanding their tweet and shouting 'SURELY THAT IS A EUPHEMISM' back 250+ times. If you want to feel like a massive unoriginal doofus, do a quick search on their name after you've sent that killer reply.

Q. But, hang on, I've looked at this celeb's replies and sometimes their tweet only gets five responses. Why are they not replying? I just know we have tons in common!

A. To be blunt, most celebrities end up slightly terrified of real people. Celebs know through experience that their face having appeared on a box in the corner of people's living rooms makes normal people act a bit wonky. Dear reader, I'm certain you and I don't behave like this, but many lesser mortals do. 'Normals' tweet 'famouses', and then the moment they get a response they put their hand out wanting something. They want sponsorship money, they want help with a life dilemma, they want a prize for their child's school raffle, they want you to watch a YouTube clip of their son juggling and to email it to Simon Cowell. They act infatuated. They send suggestive messages, then call a newspaper and tell them they're being hit on. They act like normal people for a few tweets and then when they don't get what they want they suddenly turn toxic. Celebrities end up talking to other celebs because it feels safer.

Q. But my celebrity tweeter replied once. Why was this different?

A. Sometimes tweeters catch a celebrity just as they're sitting down with a cup of coffee and time on their hands and just happened to tweet something which strikes a chord with them. 'I really loved you in *<insert name of obscure film they acted in>* when you said *<insert line that they loved saying>*.' And the celeb's eyes widen and they think, 'God, I'm so glad someone liked that!' And they reply. If this happens, why not try BEING COOL? Don't immediately bang 'favourite' on the tweets and then RT with the comment 'OMG THIS IS THE BEST MOMENT OF MY LIFE EVER!' generating a snowball effect of all your friends RTing it, honking 'WOO HOO! CONGRATULATIONS YOU HAVE WANTED THIS FOREVER AND EVER!' The celeb will read this and be a bit freaked out and slam the ANTI-LOONY portcullis in place again.

Q. I sometimes send shitty tweets to a celeb, but they have 37k followers, so surely they don't see it?

A. Tweeting nasty messages to famous tweeters' accounts is much more likely to put you on the radar of a celeb. From talking to famous folk, it appears that anyone with approximately 100k or fewer followers tends to see the abuse sent to them every day, and it does hurt them. If your purpose in life is to hurt someone's feelings, albeit momentarily, and make the world a slightly uglier place, then, yes, do tweet as this is what you're achieving. You might think, 'Oh well, they can't see it,' but if someone showed you a list of 250 messages and 249 of them said, 'Hello!' and 'How's it going today?' and one of them said, 'YOU FUCKING USELESS DICK LOSE SOME WEIGHT,' I guarantee your eye would stop on the insult, instantly forgetting the nice tweets.

Q. If celebs don't want to read bad stuff about them, then they shouldn't search their own name. Surely that means they deserve it?

A. This is partially true. If you haven't @ added their name in it, then how did they see it? The answer is they were either searching their name or, also very likely, they probably had it forwarded to them. Some tweeters make it their business to spend all day forwarding nasty tweets to the celeb's account as soon as they see them. And they don't even think they are doing anything remotely odd.

Q. My favourite celeb has suddenly left Twitter. Why?

A. It could be due to a busy diary but it's more than likely abuse problems. Whoever they are, they don't really deserve shit. Now, I'm not remotely famous – I'm in the 'sort of a bit known to a niche audience' category – but if I sit at my laptop writing a column, chatting on Skype to my brother, watching *EastEnders*, with TweetDeck open swapping tittle-tattle tweets with other Albert Square fans, I get all sorts of bleak things sent to me. There have been tweets from a man pretending to be a prolific rapist threatening to attack me, many threats to beat me up, general abuse about every square inch of my appearance, mirror accounts mimicking me and causing trouble with my friends, and other fun stuff. I can't imagine what it's like actually being properly, enormously famous, but I can imagine that if a person is feeling very wounded, Twitter is the last place they'd want to hang out.

@gracedent's advice kiosk

Dear @gracedent

Fuckin' celebs, they reckon they're it. They sit there being all chummy with each other and the minute you tweet something honest to them they get all defensive cos their IVORY TOWER has been invaded by us, the LITTLE PEOPLE. Like the other night that Sarah Sparkle off that gardening show was on Twitter talking to her mates about *EastEnders* and everyone was laughing at her jokes and kissing her arse so I tweeted, 'Why don't you get your fucking nose fixed you ugly HORE?' Well, she doesn't like this. Probably a shock to her system after all the bumlicking she's used to. So, get this, then she replies to me going, 'I think it's spelled "Whore".' Snotty cow, correcting my spelling!! So I damn well RT'd it right cos I want everyone to see that she's a silly cow who can't take any criticism, and at the end of the day, she shouldn't put herself in the public eye if she don't want people to have a pop, should she? Then I send her another tweet going 'LOL touched a nerve did i big nose bitch!!' hahahahah.

Well, then she blocked me. She blocked me? Like so much for freedom of speech, innit? Well, I looked at her timeline and she had replied to a few folk saying she was a bit down about what I'd said, then she logged off Twitter. So I told me missus and her mates and they were all pure disgusted about Sarah Sparkle taking the piss out of my spelling, so they all tweeted her messages calling her snobby slag. But she ain't replied as she's not been on Twitter for a week now. Dunnno why, probably out fucking buying a Rolls Royce or summat with all her cash that

WE THE FANS give her. Actually, I don't even know what she does. Is she a singer?

A. Cretin

Dear Mr Cretin

Well, quite. Quite.

@gracedent

Dear @gracedent

I really love my favourite celeb on Twitter and I read their tweets and all their friends' tweets every day and love hearing them chatter, but the celeb will not follow me and I have asked them lots of times and I have mailed their fansite and asked them why and told them it makes me cross and they didn't reply, so then I mailed them again and told them I was not happy with how they behave and pointing out that other people (my friends) had noticed too and I was let down by them, and they didn't reply to that too and I am really angry now and I hate them now.

Yours Sincerely

@lividlucy

Dear @lividlucy

Dude, you need to chill out and get some fresh air. Stop watching Twitter all day and night like it's a mini soap opera. A false intimacy has set in between you and a lot of people you don't even know and it's affecting your ability to reason. It might be time for a Twitter holiday, or even to think about leaving Twitter altogether. See the next chapter.

@gracedent

How to leave Twitter

Some reasons it might be time to leave Twitter (or at least take a short holiday, let's not go mad here)

Do any of the following thoughts feel familiar?

– Can you no longer see the point of experiences/emotions if you can't tweet them? 'I'm at the top of a mountain, the view is incredible!' Well, why not look at it? 'Finally cleared my inbox, now listening to Chopin with a bottle of ale. SHEER BLISS!' Not true: you're sat crouched like a gibbon over a mobile-phone screen – you can't be alone with your own thoughts for more than 60 seconds now. It could be time to leave Twitter.

– Do you only exist on Twitter? Is your entire persona basically a web of signifiers constructed via tweets? Does your self-esteem come mainly from your follower-count? Are you terrified that if you don't tweet for one whole day you'll be nothing and no-one again, and will have undone all of your good Twitter work? DUDE, IT'S TIME TO TAKE A TWITTER BREAK.

– Are you becoming more verbose to get attention, yet in fact getting less attention? Did no-one enjoy those tweets about your mid-cycle mucus? What about all the middle-of-the-night shouting about 'getting pussy'? Who wouldn't love that? Hang on, what's that noise? It's the Twitter Vacation Train, and you need to be on it.

– Are you are plainly and unarguably spending more time on your Twitter friendships than on your real partner and your own children, and they've called you out on it? Have you got to the point where you actually don't really care? Does Twitter allow you to be a far better person than you can be in real adult life with all its boring responsibilities? Because if this means destroying all the other stuff, then you're not sure you care any more . . . WOAH! LISTEN TO YOURSELF. GET OFF TWITTER. NOW.

– Have you have developed a Twitter crush and it's being reciprocated? Are the collective hormonal surges causing you both to flirt outrageously back and forth, back and forth, which everyone can see even though you think you're being so bloody subtle, and this isn't even getting into the DM conversations which led to grubby bouts of twanking? Are you in a relationship already? Do you realise that people can press 'see conversation' on one of your replies to each other and the trail of peacock strutting with all its dates and times documented is muckier and more filled with filth and longing than a stained copy of *Lady Chatterley's Lover*? You both need to get off Twitter. You can talk to each other in the Holiday Express when you both live out of bin-liners there.

– Are lots of your brilliant ideas being ripped off Twitter and turning up elsewhere? Oh, if you're good, they certainly will be. People are shameless. Those wry observations on modern life, your best puns, carefully honed one-liners, your political thoughts (which should be a thesis), that synopsis for a novel, your idea for an exhibition, your tip-off about the next big thing you keep meaning to blog about but never get round to doing – if you tweet it to the world in 140 characters, don't be surprised if someone else steals it, does it and passes it off as their own without so much as a backwards glance. Creative types love Twitter, but your intellectual property rights are about as strong as if you'd written the idea on a toilet wall. When the muse strikes hard, you need to get off Twitter.

– Do all your ideas about life come from what other people are telling you on Twitter and none from your own skull? Do you know what you even believe any more? Have you tried turning off Twitter and letting your brain go off-road and form its own opinions that have nothing to do with what your favourite tweeters think? They never need know about it as you'll never tell them. Have you thought of a Twitter break?

– Has your mother/boss/client joined Twitter and arrived in your timeline among your friends to harangue you to get off Twitter and reply to their emails? The moment people think they can harangue you about deadlines/personal duties on Twitter – well, the party is sort of over. You can either live your life as a saintly deadline-hitting goody-two-shoes prefect who never tweets about getting wasted on a school night, or you need to find somewhere else to hang out.

– Are you arguing on Twitter a lot? Do you stay awake until 3am shouting at neocons and animal experimenters and people who don't like Muse or appreciate *Doctor Who*? Have you not realised that arguing on the internet is like pulling a drunk's trousers back up for him in public? You might be on the side of righteousness but you both still look fucking stupid. Have you stopped rolling with the punches on Twitter? Are some arguments making you genuinely upset for days on end? Have you looked out of the window? Fresh air, go and smell some.

– Is Twitter making you show signs of depression? Are

you tired, ill, non-specifically blue or slightly paranoid? Are you increasingly anxious about Twitter situations with people you don't actually have contact with in real life? Are you beginning to see messages 'between the lines' that possibly aren't really there? Have you started perceiving people not replying to you as a conspiracy? Have you begun posting weird, passive-aggressive tweets saying things like 'SOMEONE PROBABLY THINKS I DON'T KNOW THEY'RE SLAGGING ME OFF BUT I DO'? OK, I don't need to tell you this, but it's time for a Twitter sabbatical.

– Have you become a Twitter troll/stalker of one or more people? Are you unable to stop yourself setting up fake accounts with only a blank anonymous 'egg' avatar just to prod them a little bit more? Are you pretty sure you won't get caught as you've done it a few times but nothing has happened? Has it occurred to you that it only really needs a collection of your tweets to be given to the right person with internet investigating skills and it would take about an hour tops to find out who you are? Does it make you feel a bit shivery when I tell you the last time I saw a friend stand up to a constant troll, it required a tiny amount of rooting about to throw up, in one fell swoop, the troll's Facebook page, his Google profile, a link to a university meet-up page for him, including the emails of his uni chums, a link to a family picture-library account, a link to his personal Flickr account, a link to his mother's 'what we're up to' blog, and all this along with his actual home address, his work email, his CEO's email and details of his interests and hobbies. Our muddy footprints are all over the internet; no-one is truly anonymous. So please carry on being the silent wanking egg-troll person if you want, but maybe, here's a thought, maybe you need to get off Twitter.

– Do you feel that, although you agree with many of the statements above, you can never, ever leave Twitter? Oh, calm down, Doris, and stop being so dramatic. Let's start with 72 hours . . .

How to leave Twitter

Are you ready to give a Twitter-free life a go? Follow these simple, straightforward sections in this order. Do not skip a stage. If you don't complete a stage, return to the beginning.

1. The 'delusions of own importance' stage

I can't leave Twitter. People will miss me. Why, if they don't hear my sanguine observations on modern life how will the world spin? And what about my hilarious spoof character I do which brings solid LOLZ to so many timelines? And all the breaking news I bring and political revolutions I work as a small cog in a giant wheel to ignite. Oh, what will happen to the Twittersphere without lovely me?

Answer: nothing. People will just read other people's tweets for a while. Almost everyone will assume you're on holiday or busy or won't notice you're not there at all.

2. The 'I need to say my goodbyes' stage

One way to never, ever leave Twitter is to tell people you are leaving Twitter. It's very much like trying to leave a party before midnight by stopping the music and asking everyone where your coat is and for the number of a good minicab firm. People will try everything to stop you going. 'Are you tired, have another drink, you don't need to go, just have a soft drink, come and dance, do you want drugs, we're getting a taxi later, you've not met Cyril and he's amazing, oh please stay, we only came out for you.' Twitter is a lot like this, but with none of the booze or the drugs or meeting Cyril; just people imploring you not to go as they want you to be like them and spend 16 hours a day staring at Twitter.com. DON'T SAY GOODBYE. JUST GO.

3. The 'removing the party in your pocket' stage

You are now going to bin the Twitter application on your mobile phone. It will take about three seconds. Try to experiment with leaving your mobile phone on a high shelf in the house and only paying it attention when it actually rings with a telephone call from someone with something valid they need to say to you.

4. The 'ceremonious binning of Twitter client off your laptop' stage

Yes, I know this is severe, but if you've got this far in the book it suggests to me you can't be trusted. Get rid of that zippy Twitter client. It will be your undoing.

5. The 'switching your password to something bloody silly' stage

Visit the Twitter main website and change your password to something very long and stupid and unmemorable. Write the new password on a piece of paper and put it in a drawer in the house. In an absolute emergency you could find it, but there will be no emergencies, unless needing desperately to tweet a YouTube clip of a Russian cat trying to cram itself into a very small box is an emergency.

6. The 'no wifi, no cry' stage

Turn off the wifi altogether for a few hours. This makes you scared, doesn't it? Embrace the fear and do it anyway. Unplug your internet router, make a nice cup of tea and sit calmly and quietly staring at a blank wall. Head detox. Turn the radio and the TV off – these will only give you things to think about or be cross about or that make you crave to tweet about. Start to allow questions about the world to cross your brain, questions to which you have no answers and cannot Google or ask of Twitter. Let yourself rely simply on your own powers of logic, rumination and reckoning. Experiment with thoughts not needing to do anything other than circumnavigate your mind, that never need be expressed on the internet.

7. The 'notice things going on within your own four walls' stage

Begin some light 'pottering' around your home, sorting out things within your own four walls, instead of ranging all over the cyber-world putting out fires and starting other ones.

You may notice that your house is mucky and has several jammy, fuzzy surfaces that may need disinfecting. Why not hang that framed print that's been in the hall since 2009? Or sort your cutlery drawer out, sterilise some tea-cups, attack your house cushions with a Bobble-be-gone shaver. Open the fridge and remove anything with a sell-by date in the Triassic period and/or a mould beard. Go out to the garden and prune something back, breathing lungfuls of air. Do you feel good? DO NOT GO AND FIND YOUR TWITTER PASSWORD IN THE DRAWER AND TWEET DROLL COMMENTS ABOUT BEING 'A DOMESTIC GODDESS'. You have not left Twitter if you pop back on to Twitter to tweet about your success.

8. The bargaining stage

'But I need to go on Twitter to organise my night out with my friend. And I need to get a recipe that someone tweeted in my timeline. And I need to say hello Boris in Bolton as his goldfish was on its way out and he'll be blue. And I always look at Twitter during the football scores. And what if I just go on Twitter for 20 minutes before bed to get a gist of the day's events? And what if I only check it on your phone and not mine? And . . .'

No. No exceptions. There's no halfway house between being on and off Twitter. That's why you're in this mess.

9. The 'boo-boo where are you' stage

After 24 hours you may begin to receive the odd seemingly frantic (translation: nosy) email asking why you have left. Was it something they said? Have you officially left? Did you know that someone else on Twitter thinks they have offended you? Do you know that people miss you and have been asking after you? Reply politely but do not engage in Twitter gossip, and if necessary eat the piece of paper with the password on it so you have to wait for five hours for it to come out the other end.

10. The recovering Twitter addict stage

Is your head less cluttered now? Are you sleeping more deeply and waking more refreshed? Is your house cleaner now and less like Dr Terrible's House of Horrible? Do your children not look puzzled when you speak to them any more? Is the divorce off (for now)? Did granny get a birthday card on time? Do you own normal, flappy, pliable hands like calm people now and not scrunched-up angry 'I have been arguing all morning on the internet' fists? Is your attention span slowly returning to more than 2.7 seconds per topic? Is Twitter not the boss of you any more?

Oh god, this feeling is magical, isn't it? Quitting Twitter is so invigorating. I love it so much I've done it 117 times. And each and every time, within days or at the most weeks, I have broken my pledge, reinstalled TweetDeck, loaded the app back on to my iPhone and sneaked back on, only to find the territory even more intoxicating than ever before. Oh, Twitter. You terrible, brilliant, inescapable thing. Your demure, blank 'What's happening?' box, needing the cerebral challenge of a killer 140 character zing. The hypnotic nature of dragging links into tweets, the satisfying buzz of watching them shorten, the unquantifiable pleasure of finding the perfect Google picture to illustrate a joke. The timeline and mentions column filling up with notes from friends in far-flung places with fake names gabbing about abstract things. And now I've been away, don't my fingers feel extra-zingy as they tippy-tap-tap along the keyboard, and don't these DMs no-one else can read feel all the more delicious? And don't I feel less like Grace the girl who needs to load the dishwasher and more like 'Grace, Queen of the Universe'?

And, yes, one day I plan to leave Twitter definitely and forever, and figure out a way to put the genie back in the bottle, to live my life tolerably and patiently at a quarter of the speed, using one brain and not a collective consciousness of more than 200 million tweeters. But until then, if you have any good ideas, please tweet me any time, day or night, this week, next month and for the foreseeable future on @gracedent at www.twitter.com.

Acknowledgements

The wondrous Lisa Darnell for prodding me to do this. My brilliant agent Karolina Sutton at Curtis Brown. Jon Wilkinson for his patience. Emma Freud, without whom this would never have been finished. Julian Loose at Faber for staying calm. Geno, who was, as ever, a great help, and Poppy.